The Cross Timbers

MEMORIES OF A NORTH TEXAS BOYHOOD

Personal Narratives of the West

J. Frank Dobie, General Editor

The Cross Timbers

MEMORIES OF A NORTH TEXAS BOYHOOD

by Edward Everett Dale

Illustrated by John Biggers

UNIVERSITY OF TEXAS PRESS
AUSTIN

Library of Congress Catalog Card No. 65–27540
Copyright © 1966 by Edward Everett Dale
All Rights Reserved

First paperback printing, 2012

ISBN 978-0-292-74069-3

To Judy and Everett
whose childhood differed so much from my own

PREFACE

This story of my boyhood in the Texas Cross Timbers has been written largely from memory, although old letters and other family documents have been consulted to verify dates and some events.

Whether the story is worth telling is a matter of opinion, but it reveals a pattern of life in rural America now gone forever. Moreover, it is not my story alone. Except for some minor variations due to climate and other geographic conditions, it is largely the life story of a vast number of other boys who lived on a woodland farm in the period from 1882 to 1892. Perhaps this is its chief value, for we are largely what the past has made us, and to some extent it is true that "the child is father to the man."

To all those who have given me encouragement and help in the work of preparing this little volume for publication I want to express my sincere thanks and deep appreciation. My special thanks are due to my secretaries, Judy Kaye Moore, Mrs. R. L. Pettett, and Loretta Sue Pillow, who typed the manuscript, and to my wife, Rosalie, who gave much aid in its revision and was often a patient listener.

Edward Everett Dale
Norman, Oklahoma

CONTENTS

The Cross Timbers

MEMORIES OF A NORTH TEXAS BOYHOOD

Introduction

It is commonly said that the youngest child in a family is always hopelessly spoiled. If this is true I entered the world under a terrific handicap, for it was my fate to be the youngest of my father's twelve children. Two of these died in childhood, but most of the remaining ten lived to a ripe old age.

As the youngest, I had the good fortune to be born in Texas. My father was born in Kentucky on January 28, 1829, but in 1831 his Virginia-born father migrated with his family to Northwest Missouri, where he settled near Richmond, in Ray County.

Here my father grew to manhood and in 1850 joined the gold rush to California, walking all the way beside the oxen that drew his covered wagon. After a year of digging gold, with only modest success, he returned home by way of Panama and married Louisa Colley, whose family had migrated from Virginia to Ray County, Missouri, by way of the Ohio and Missouri Rivers.

Their first son, Henry, was born a year after their marriage and eventually five more sons and four daughters were born of this marriage, but one son and a daughter died in early childhood. Some years after the close of the Civil War, Louisa Colley Dale died; after a decent interval Father married her younger sister, Mattie Counts Colley, who became my mother five years after the birth of her first child—my brother George.

Soon after George's birth my father and his younger brother, Isaac sold their land in Missouri and removed with their families to Nebraska, settling on Rock Creek about sixteen miles northeast of Lincoln. Here they took land under the Homestead Act of Congress, built homes, broke the prairie sod, and planted crops, but the cold winters and a plague of grasshoppers caused them to remove to Texas after three or four years in Nebraska.

My father reached the Lone Star State with all his family except Henry, who had a farm in Nebraska. The following spring the Nebraska sweetheart of the oldest daughter, Fannie, came to Texas to marry her and take her back to his home on Rock Creek. About the same time Father's second son, Frank, returned to Lincoln to enter the University of Nebraska. In the meantime my father had rented for a term of three years a prairie farm in Tarrant County, two or three miles west of the edge of the Lower Cross Timbers. It was in the comfortable frame house on this farm that I was born on February 8, 1879, slightly less than three years before my father moved us to our new home in the Cross Timbers.

The origin of the term "Cross Timbers" is obscure. We only know that during most of the nineteenth century it was applied to the two broad belts of timber that extended northward from Central Texas to the Red River and far beyond. The eastern belt, called the Lower Cross Timbers, was separated from the western belt, or Upper Cross Timbers, by a strip of blackland prairie, eight or nine miles wide where we lived, but much wider farther south. In the early spring this green prairie became a gorgeous carpet of wild flowers.

The eastern edge of the Lower Cross Timbers was slightly west of Sherman and Dallas, while its western boundary was not far from the main line of the Missouri, Kansas, and Texas Railway. Obviously, the boundary was jagged and broken. Long "peninsulas" of woodland extended out into the prairie and small "islands" of trees were common, usually on top of a low hill surrounded by grasslands.

In marked contrast to the rich, black soil of the prairie, that of the Cross Timbers was thin and sandy, with occasional outcroppings of clay. In a few places there were heavy flat stones, which the children called "iron rocks" to indicate their weight and to distinguish them from the red sandstone found in some places where rain had washed away the soil.

The trees in this area included the blackjack, which seldom grew to a height of over thirty feet. Usually they were found on rough rocky land, and were sometimes called "poor-land trees." On the level sandy land grew the post oaks, which might reach a height of fifty or sixty feet. On some of the sandy flats the principal trees were hickory, while along the small streams they were elm, cottonwood, hackberry, walnut, pecan, and chinaberry.

Naturally, the youngsters of the Cross Timbers were most interested in the trees and smaller plants which produced something edible. Of these there was a wide variety, including dewberries, blackberries, mulberries, three or four kinds of plums, persimmons, black haws, red haws, and at least three varieties of grapes. The mustang grapevines sometimes climbed to the top of tall trees. Other types of grapes were the winter or "possum grapes," not ripening until late autumn, and sand-beach grapes.

Both blackjack and post-oak trees produced quantities of acorns, which pigs ate greedily, but which were too bitter for human consumption. Therefore, the only nut-producing trees were pecan, hickory, and walnut.

Other plants of interest to adults were found in these woods. Redroot, horehound, and stillingia were said to have much medicinal value. Housewives often picked lamb's-quarter, poke leaves, and dock leaves to be boiled and eaten as "wild greens." There were also plants to be avoided, such as poison oak, poison ivy, stinging nettles, the big bull nettles, and sand burrs. Most children seemed to be immune to poison ivy and poison oak but many adults were not.

With the exception of cottontail rabbits, fox squirrels, and 'possums, few wild animals lived in the Cross Timbers. A few raccoons and skunks could be found, and possibly a fox or a prairie wolf might be seen once in a period of ten years. The big jack rabbits were found mostly on the prairie. There were snakes, but the only poisonous ones were the copperheads. Many birds of various kinds lived in the Cross Timbers, including the big turkey buzzards, crows, mockingbirds, shrikes, quails, turtle-doves, meadow larks, bluebirds, several kinds of hawks, blue jays with their bright-blue coats and white underclothes, hoot owls, screech owls, whippoorwills, and woodpeckers.

It was my privilege to live in the Lower Cross Timbers for ten years. Looking backward over three quarters of a century, I see it now as an excellent place for a growing boy to have lived, as I did from the age of three to thirteen.

1. Be It Ever So Humble

One evening when I was about four years old we had supper a little later than usual, and at its conclusion my father said that he believed he'd walk over to Jim McCarty's home to return a spade he had borrowed, adding that he might stay and visit for an hour or so. The rest of us, consisting of my mother and half-sister Mattie, who was then about sixteen, my brother, George, aged about ten, and myself, lingered at the table.

The atmosphere cleared a little when Father was gone, for though all of us had for him the highest respect and a deep affection, he was a dignified and fairly stern father, so we usually felt some constraint in his presence. He had had twelve children and a family of that size must be managed somewhat like an institution. In consequence, he demanded respectful and prompt obedience from the younger generation and frowned upon their manifesting any symptoms of what the old-time Puritans referred to as "light carriage."

Upon this particular occasion I was sitting on a bench behind the table, Mattie was opposite me, and Mother at the foot of the table near the stove was telling some stories of her girlhood days in Missouri. Said she:

One morning in October two boys came to our house. The older seemed to be about twelve and the other was a little fellow not much bigger than

Ed here. They had run away from home and it had rained the night before, so they had slept in a straw stack but were wet, cold, and hungry. The larger boy said he was looking for a job with someone who would let him keep his little brother with him. The little fellow had been crying and I felt so sorry for him, but we had no work for his brother to do. We brought them in and gave them a good breakfast and they went on with the older one saying that he just had to find work.

Apparently no one had been paying any attention to me, sitting behind the table and trying to make letters of the alphabet with my knife, fork, and spoon. When my mother concluded, however, I spoke up with a little sob in my throat, "You bet I never will wun away and leave my home ath long ath there'th a pieth of it left that big," and I held up a small thumb indicating to what tiny dimensions my home must shrink before it should cease to be blessed by my presence.

George and Mattie laughed loudly, but my mother rose and came over to put her arms around my shoulders and whispered that she was glad I loved my home and did not want to leave it. She then added that she hoped I would someday have a home of my own that would be just as happy as this one. Thirty-five years were to elapse before this hope of my mother's was realized.

This home to which I had pledged such undying devotion was a fifty-six–acre farm located at the western edge of the Lower Cross Timbers of Texas. The term "farm" is used because at this time and place a home was far more than the residence in which a family lived. It included not only "the orchard, the meadow, the deep tangled wildwood" but the barns, cribs, garden, fields, pastures, and fences. The house, to the kids at least, was only more or less incidental, and in good weather they stayed inside it just as little as possible.

Our house stood on a tree-crowned hill near the center of the little farm and faced the west. From the front door we had a magnificent view of the broad, flower-spangled prairie, which lay beyond the railroad that skirted the western border of the farm. The original house was built of logs and consisted of only two rooms and an attic bedroom reached by a sort of combination of ladder and stairway. When I was about three, however, my father had added on the north a large kitchen built of lumber, where we cooked and ate. It was furnished with a big wood stove with a kitchen table beside it, and the large dining table covered with oilcloth except if "company" came, at which time a white or red tablecloth was spread over it. In addition, there were two or three chairs with rawhide seats and a tall cupboard called a "safe," where the dishes and leftover food were stored. With respect to food, however, the term "safe" was something of a misnomer with a couple of ever-hungry boys in the house.

The small rear room was Mattie's and had her bed and a couple of trunks that held linens, shirts, and underwear. Outer clothing was hung on nails driven in the walls, while surplus bedding was stacked on two or three shelves.

The large "front room," as we called it, had a big stone fireplace on the north side and from each corner of the mantle was hung a glass tumbler in a crocheted mesh bag. These held buttons, pins, needles and thread, and other small objects. The big bed of my father and mother stood in the southeast corner of the room. It was covered with a white counterpane and had a bolster and two large pillow shams.

A small trundle bed on rollers was kept under this big bed by day and rolled out at night. I slept on this until I was four or five years old, but then demanded permission to sleep with George upstairs in the attic. A couple of rag rugs on the floor, a rocker or two, and three or four straight chairs completed the furnishing of this principal room of the house. The problem of storage was in part solved by a big cellar in the back yard, where my mother kept milk, butter, and jars of canned fruit, preserves, and pickles. There were also bins for the storage of turnips, sweet potatoes, and other vegetables.

Some distance south of the house were pole-fenced lots for the horses and pigs, and sheds, stables, and corn cribs. Our front door opened upon a small porch from which a path led to the front-yard gate. On either side of this path was a Russian mulberry tree and flowers, including zinnias, phlox, pinks, and iris— then commonly called "flags." North of the house was the garden and beyond it an orchard of more than a hundred trees, mostly peach, but with a few apple, pear, cherry, and plum trees.

This fifty-six–acre tract of land was only three miles east of the prairie farm which my father had rented a few months after his arrival in Texas. He had bought it about a year or so after moving onto the rented place from Ike Roberts, an old cowman whose father had received a large land grant in this area from the Texas Republic. Ike had inherited this grant at his father's death and was selling it in tracts of a size to suit the purchaser. He still retained a huge acreage, however, on which his cattle grazed, as did the milk cows of the nearby farmers since most of his pasture land was not fenced. His home was a large ranch house on top of a small tree-covered knoll, well out on the prairie and commonly called "Brushy Mound."

When my father bought this little parcel of land it was covered with timber, largely blackjack, but with many large post-oak trees which could be used in building a house and out buildings. During the years before the lease expired on the prairie farm he spent every day that could be spared from growing and harvesting crops to improving his new property. He cut down the larger trees and squared the logs for the house and barns, cleared away the underbrush, and planted an orchard.

When a field had been cleared he enclosed it, in Indian fashion, with a brush fence, pending the time when he could split enough rails to replace this with a rail fence. At times it must have seemed an almost hopeless task, for after the trees had been felled the stumps must be grubbed out with a mattock, or "grubbing hoe." Moreover, the forest fought back in a most stubborn fashion, for sprouts persistently sprang up in a desperate attempt to resist the work of man and again "let in the jungle." He never despaired, however, and just before I was three years old he moved us into our new log house and soon added the large kitchen.

Most of the people in our community, and throughout the Texas Cross Timbers, had homes like ours, except perhaps for the big orchard. Some of our neighbors, however, had much larger houses, especially if they had large families of children, but it must be confessed that there was little relationship between the size of a family and that of its living quarters. The Clarks, who owned a twenty-acre farm joining ours on the east, had five children, but lived for some years in a crude, two-room log house before adding another room at a cost of forty dollars!

It must be admitted that our little house would be considered very small today, but in the 1880's it seemed quite adequate for a family of five. All my father's older children were grown up and out on their own. The first and second sons, Henry and Frank, and the oldest daughter, Fannie, were in Nebraska. The third son, Tom, had married Lucy, the youngest daughter of an old Texan of the neighborhood who had deeded the young couple a farm about a mile southeast of ours. Alice, the middle daughter, had a job in a Dallas hospital. As to the other two sons, Jay was bookkeeper for a large general merchandise store at Fort Griffin,

Texas, and his younger brother, John, was teaching school near that little frontier post.

Humble as was our little home, it was a very happy one. My father worked from dawn to dark improving the farm, and my mother was a remarkably good cook who prepared excellent meals, sometimes from quite meager resources, and kept every room neat and clean. Most of the food came from the farm, since we had milk cows, chickens, and pigs. The orchard and garden furnished an ample supply of fruit and vegetables, and half a dozen stands of bees yielded plenty of honey.

Our greatest difficulty was a lack of water for household use. Father had dug two wells and although he struck a plentiful supply of clear, cool water at a depth of about thirty feet, it tasted as though the contents of a family medicine chest had been dumped into it. Just what minerals it had in solution we never knew, for no one in the community had ever heard of water analysis. Strangers who were called upon for information tasted it, made a face, and guessed that it might be saltpeter, gypsum, or any other mineral of which they knew.

As a result, we were forced to haul water in barrels from a big spring half a mile away or from the well of our nearest neighbor. A small stock pond was built in the hog pasture to supply water for the livestock, but in time of drought we sometimes rode the horses to the spring to water them. We also often took the family washing to the spring or the neighbor's well on "washday."

The railroad which ran along the western edge of my father's farm was the Missouri, Kansas, and Texas. On it, a mile and a half south of us, was the little village of Keller. This was our nearest town though Roanoke was only three miles north of our home. Fifteen miles south of Keller was Fort Worth, at that time a little city of perhaps thirty thousand. I never visited it, however, until after I was eight years old. In fact a trip to that city was something to be considered carefully, and almost prayerfully, for a journey of sixteen and a half miles in a farm wagon was quite an adventure. One was forced to start at dawn and seldom got back until after dark. Besides, my father felt that the relationship between Fort Worth and ancient Sodom was much the same as that between Minneapolis and St. Paul—a feeling which at that time may have had some justification!

In the fall of 1884 Henry sold his Nebraska farm and came to Texas to spend the winter with us. He drove down with a new wagon and a team of large horses and considerable money in his pocket. He had developed a great interest in photography and promptly bought a couple of cameras and materials for developing pictures.

Obviously, no one in the community had any money to buy photographs, but he made many tintypes and other photographs of members of the family. These he touched up with paint until we looked like Indians ready for the warpath. He put gold rings on our fingers and, if not bells on our toes, brooches and watch chains on blouses and vests that had never known such adornment. When winter was over he gave up the venture and drove out to the Wichita Falls and Vernon, Texas, area to engage in freighting, hunting, and trapping.

Mattie had spent part of the fall and winter of 1884–1885 at Fort Griffin visiting Jay, who had secured a room for her at the home of his landlady. She must have had a wonderful time attending parties and socials in this little frontier town, where the

coming of an attractive young girl was an event of major importance. Here she made many friends, including the young man
she was to marry later.

Jay's employers not only owned the large general merchandise
establishment for which he was bookkeeper but also had exten-
sive ranching interests and some manufacturing enterprises in
Mexico. In the spring of 1885 they were sending a herd of 2,500
steers north to a range in North Dakota. Jay, tired of indoor life,
asked them to give his brother John and him a job on this
northern drive.

With some reluctance they agreed and the two brothers made
the long drive to the range of the Long X Ranch near that of
Theodore Roosevelt. Here Jay remained for a year, but the following summer his employers offered him the job of bookkeeper
for a cottonseed-oil mill and soap factory they owned in Tamau-
lipas, Mexico, and he gladly accepted. Later that summer Mattie
returned to Fort Griffin to visit friends there and soon wrote that
she had married the young man she had met the preceding winter.

That fall came the death of my mother. She was a sweet-faced,
gentle woman, too frail perhaps for the hard life of the American
frontier of that time. Her health had been bad for two or three
years, but she was always cheerful and happy and was never
confined to her bed.

For some reason I was sleeping on the little trundle bed in the
back bedroom when I was awakened by George shaking my
shoulder and saying, "Oh, Ed, poor old Ma is dead, we won't
ever get to see her any more."

I sat up with my eyes heavy with sleep not quite able to realize
the tragedy that had befallen us. Then my father came in and

kissed me gently and went out. I got up and dressed; while going through the living room to the kitchen I saw a sheet spread over something on the bed which I knew must be my mother's body. Lucy and a couple of other women were in the kitchen, while George was outside doing the chores, and Father had gone to Keller for a casket.

The women fixed me some breakfast and when George had finished with feeding the livestock, he was sent to notify two or three of the neighbors and I trailed along. When we reached the first house George knocked at the door and when a woman opened it he said, "They sent me over to ask if you'd come over and help us a little. Ma died last night and we need a little help."

The shocked look on the woman's face as George made his simple announcement is still vivid in my memory. She replied that she would be right over and George and I went on to take our message to a couple of other neighbors.

When we reached home, she and three or four other neighbor women were there. Some of them had brought their children, who were playing about in the yard. On the little porch before the front door an old woman sat in a rocking chair picking out the seeds from a pile of cotton in her lap to make a little pillow for my mother's head. I went inside and saw a long black box with shining handles, which I knew was the coffin to hold her body.

I joined the other children at play in the yard while the women inside the house, with rough, toil-worn hands, prepared the body for burial and cooked dinner and supper. Most of them then returned to their homes, but three or four men and women remained to watch throughout the night, as was the universal custom.

The next afternoon the casket was placed in a wagon, and we all drove to the little Bourland Cemetery, where Reverend Bourland conducted a brief funeral service. The casket was then lowered into the grave which willing neighbors filled. Then my father, George, and I, accompanied by Tom and Lucy, returned to our little house which seemed strangely empty and lonely. The next day, however, Alice resigned her job in the hospital and came home to keep house for us.

2. Neighbors and Visitors

It is fortunate that children seldom brood long over a tragic loss or great sorrow. George and I loved our mother dearly but her passing made little change in the normal pattern of our lives. Our sister Alice, who was a fairly large blonde woman, took over the management of the little household with expert hands.

She was a good cook, an excellent housekeeper, and so much older than ourselves that we accorded to her the same respect that we had always given to our mother. In fact, courtesy to older persons had been taught me so thoroughly since earliest childhood that my practice of it proved a bit embarrassing sometimes in later life, when some people thought me old-fashioned.

Upon one occasion I heard someone calling me from the next room. Thinking it was George, I yelled, "What!" Unfortunately it was my father, who came in frowning as he asked, "What do you mean by answering me like that? Isn't that a pretty way for a boy to talk to his father? You say 'Sir' when you speak to me."

I could only reply in stammering fashion that I thought it had been George calling me, which was the Gospel truth.

Long before the death of my mother I had developed something of a local reputation for singing and quoting verse. This was probably due to my lisping voice and inability to pronounce the letter *s*. One of my favorite songs was the old ballad about Sam Bass, the Texas outlaw, whose center of operation had been the town of Denton, about twenty miles north of our home. My own version of the first two stanzas was as follows:

> Ham Bath wath born in Indiana-a-a,
> It wath hith native home
> And at the age of heventeen
> Young Ham began to roam.
> He firth came out to Texath
> A team-ter for to be
> A kinder hearted fellow
> You heldom ever hee.
>
> 'Tarted with a herd of Texath cattle
> The Black Hillth for to hee
> Arrived at the town of Denton
> And there got on a 'pree
> Hold out in Cuther Hity
> And there got on a 'pree
> A tougher het of cowboyth
> You heldom ever hee.

My love of verses or rhyming lines also came very early and is still with me. When I was a small youngster, however, this was chiefly because the ringing words of a poem appealed to me, just as did the rattling of pebbles which I put in a tin can and shook to accompany my so-called singing.

Probably the first rhyme I ever memorized must have been read to me from a Democratic newspaper soon after the presidential election in November, 1884, but it still sticks in my memory as this is written in 1965:

Blaine on a warhorse
Logan on a mule
Butler on a saw-horse
Looking like a fool.

Cleveland in the White House
Counting out his money
Hendricks in the hó-tel
Eating bread and honey.

It must be confessed that I never sang or quoted poetry when in the presence of my father or any adult visitor but only when playing or working alone or when performing for the doubtful benefit of George or kids of the neighbors.

In a so-called "horse and buggy age," though my father never owned a buggy in his life, our friends and neighbors were largely limited to persons living within a radius of three or four miles of our home. Moreover, some of the farms near us were occupied by renters, who moved frequently. As a result, in the period of ten years when we lived in the Cross Timbers three or four families might occupy a single farm, each living on it for only two or three years.

When I was about five years old, one of our neighbors, Jap Blodgett, who lived in the edge of the timber southwest of us, had to make a week's trip to Wise County, some thirty miles west of Keller. His family—consisting of his wife; a fourteen-year-old daughter, Sarah Ellen; Bill, about George's age; and Jane, about my own—were afraid to stay alone at night. Jap accordingly asked George to come and spend the nights with them while he was away, and I always tagged along. Just how much protection a boy of ten could give to them apparently never occurred to Jap.

Mrs. Blodgett insisted that we always come and have supper with the children and her. After supper we always played marbles with Bill until dark and then "fox and geese" by the light of a small brass lamp until bedtime. It was cotton-picking season, and in one corner of the so-called living room Jap had built a large pen, into which the full cotton sacks had been emptied as they were brought in from the field. The top of this pen of cotton had been leveled and quilts spread over it. Here George, Bill, and I slept every night.

When morning came and Mrs. Blodgett called that breakfast was nearly ready George and I rolled out and dressed instantly. Bill's mother never called him, but merely turned the cover back and started spanking him as she exclaimed; "Git up from there you lazy, triflin' rascal you! Breakfast is just about ready and them cows has to be milked. Git up now this minute."

Groaning and yawning, Bill would at last bestir himself and slip on his shirt and overalls. He would then snort two or three times in the washpan as he dabbed a little water on the central part of his face, dry it with a towel, and sit down to breakfast.

I can remember thinking, even this early, how different the Blodgett home was from our own. My father would never have thought of piling cotton in the house. He would either build a pen for it at the end of the field and cover it with a wagon sheet or empty the full sacks directly into the wagon in which the cotton was to be hauled to the gin. I noted too that the Blodgett home was dirty, though our own was always scrupulously clean, and that Bill said "You-uns" in speaking of George and me. This was bad to me, though Heaven knows my own use of English left much to be desired.

Jap returned to report that he had found and bought a little farm in Wise County. As soon as the crops had been harvested the Blodgetts removed to it and we never saw them again.

They were replaced by the Elstons, but they stayed only a year and we never "neighbored" with them very much. They had no children, but Mrs. Elston's nephew, George, lived with them. He was about my age and once told me that he was "an orphan and a half" because his father and mother were dead and his brother was dead!

The farm was then bought by Jake West, who lived there for many years. He and his wife, "Pet," had no children, but Pet's brother, Bob Kemp, lived with them. He was about a year older than I but we played together sometimes and both of us attended the Keller School.

Jake's teen-age sister, Evie, also visited Pet and him from time to time, often staying for several weeks. One summer evening Alice, George, and I had dropped over to the Wests' after supper to visit until bedtime. Because it was very warm, chairs were brought out to the back yard and we were sitting there talking. Soon after dark we heard an unearthly scream from the nearby trees. Both Evie and Pet were nearly scared out of their wits until investigation proved that it was only the cry of a harmless little screech owl.

"I just didn't know what it might be," said Evie apologetically, "with that child dyin' over here at Smith's just night before last."

The old superstition that the spirit of a person who had just died might hang around its familiar haunts for several days was common in many parts of America seventy-five or a hundred years ago.

Probably not many of our neighbors believed this, but some of them had other superstitions equally absurd. One day Fletcher Williams, a neighbor boy, came up when George and I were throwing rocks at a big frog at the edge of the water in the stock pond.

"Stop that!" he called excitedly. "Don't you know that if you kill a frog it will make your cows give bloody milk?"

We laughed at Fletcher to show scorn at any such idea but he still insisted that it was true. Upon another occasion I asked a

girl carrying her baby brother what was the small dark object on a string tied about the baby's neck.

"A mole's foot," she replied. "We tied it around his neck so cuttin' his teeth wouldn't be so hard for him."

George and I both scoffed at this, just as we did at old man Smith's carrying a potato in his pocket to relieve his rheumatism, but it must be confessed that we had a few superstitions of our own.

Someone had told us a yarn about an old fellow who had gone out to his watermelon patch in early spring and counted all the

little melons. Unfortunately, he had pointed his finger at each
one as he counted and the following morning found that every
one at which he had pointed had dropped off the vine! I doubt
if we really believed this but just to be on the safe side we never
pointed a finger at any baby melon, but used a stick or a fist or
foot to call attention to it!

We had also been told by some lad in the neighborhood that
if you were walking along the road and your side began to hurt,
it was easy to stop it. All you had to do was to stoop over and
pick up a small rock, turn it over, spit on it, and then replace it
with the "spit side" down and the pain in your side would be
gone. I tried this a few times and it always worked but I later
found that pausing long enough to stoop over and straighten up
brought the same relief.

Our nearest neighbor during the entire time that we lived in
the Cross Timbers was "Uncle" Jack Clark and his wife, probably
christened "Marie" but called "Mariar." The Clarks owned a
twenty-acre farm joining ours on the east. About five acres of
this was woodland, leaving only fifteen acres in cultivation minus
the space occupied by the house, yard, and out buildings. Their
family consisted of three sons and two small daughters. John,
the oldest son, was about the age of George. Bill was about my
age, and Ben a year or so younger. To provide a living for a
family of that size the Clarks needed to rent fifteen or twenty
acres of land every year from someone in the community who
owned more land than he could cultivate.

Jack was born and reared in Tennessee, but his family had
migrated to Grayson County, Texas; after marrying Mariar he
had removed westward to our neighborhood and had bought this

little farm. Since his home was only a quarter of a mile from ours we saw him and his youngsters nearly every day, for we usually hauled barrels of water for household use from his well.

He was a queer character who walked in a curious crablike, sideling fashion, possibly due to some injury or a slight stroke. Before meeting anyone he would call out, while still sixty to seventy feet away, whatever he happened to be thinking about at the moment, always followed by a "yep, yep, yep." One day George and I were walking along the road leading to Uncle Jack's house and saw him coming to meet us. When he was about twenty yards away he suddenly leaped into the air, executed half a dozen fancy dance steps and called to us, "All jine hands and skip to my Lou!—A game we used to play back in Tennessee, Georgy, yep, yep, yep. Guess you and Eddie never played it. Lots o' fun though, yep, yep, yep!"

Under the Common Law of most backwoods rural areas, including the Texas Cross Timbers, there was a curious division of property in every family. The chickens, milk cows, and garden belonged to the wife, while the horses, dogs, pigs, and farming tools were owned by the man. Usually the wife milked the cows, although a doting husband would sometimes regularly relieve her of this task. In any case, however, the "butter-and-egg" money and the proceeds from the sale of any garden vegetables were sometimes about all that the housewife had to spend as she pleased. In consequence, she diligently cared for the chickens, growing as many as possible, and insisted that the cows be well fed so that they would give plenty of milk to make enough butter for the family and some to sell.

No woman in our community was more solicitous in such

matters than Mrs. Clark. When the cows began to yield less milk she earnestly urged her husband to feed them more, and Jack responded that he would add a full feeding of cottonseed to their hitherto scanty ration of fodder. The result was miraculous. Jack, who did the milking, began to bring in each morning and evening two huge pails almost overflowing with milk instead of only a little over half-full. Yet the quantity of butter made remained the same as before. Mrs. Clark was puzzled until she at last caught Jack stopping at the well and filling the half-empty milk pails with water! Fortunately, she had a sense of humor and was so pleased with her husband's cleverness in trying to keep peace in the family that she gleefully told the story to the neighbors.

One morning Jack went out to milk and when he picked up a large bucket turned upside down on his well curb he found a big 'possum under it. The animal had been placed there the night before by some fun-loving 'possum hunters. After he had recovered from the shock Jack called his wife to come and see his strange find. As the animal stood there blinking at them Mrs. Clark remarked that it had eyes like those of their baby daughter, "Fat." This comparison caused Jack to refuse to permit the animal to be killed. Any critter with eyes like his baby girl's must be turned loose to roam the woods in peace!

One morning when we had driven over to Clark's well for a couple of barrels of water, Mrs. Clark came out to visit a few minutes and told us that when crops were laid by she was going to take the children and go "back East" to see Jack's folks.

"Where is back East?" inquired Father, thinking that she probably meant Tennessee.

"Grayson County," she replied. This was only about fifty or sixty miles northeast of our home.

"Are you going on the train?" inquired my father.

"Law no! I don't 'spect I could get any of my children nigh a train 'cept John!"

John, who was about George's age of nearly seventeen at this time, was the only one of the three Clark brothers who spoke plainly. Bill and Ben were never able to pronounce words correctly, both having a speech impediment.

A month or so later Mrs. Clark and all the youngsters, except Bill, who was left to keep his father company, started for Grayson County in a covered wagon. She had a large flock of chickens and earnestly urged Jack to take good care of them, for she wanted to sell two or three dozen fryers when she got back and also plenty of eggs later. She had set an excellent example, for she never killed a chicken for dinner except on Sunday and then only one, which supplied only a couple of pieces each for the five kids.

Jack assured his wife that he would do his best, but the wagon was hardly out of sight before he and Bill went out and started wringing chickens' necks. When we arrived at the well for two barrels of water Jack and Bill were seated at a table on the little front porch diligently eating fried chicken, and two large skillets on the stove inside were full of more being fried against the time when their well-filled plates were empty.

When Mrs. Clark and her brood returned she found her stock of poultry sadly depleted, but Jack talked convincingly of the inroads of hawks, wolves, and other varmints. Also, he and Bill, like the peasants of France before the Revolution, had carefully concealed the evidence by burying the feathers! Aunt Mariar probably had her suspicions but definite proof was lacking.

While the Clarks were sufficiently queer and ignorant to be interesting, we had other neighbors that we found more congenial. Among them were the Taylors, who owned a large farm about a half mile northeast of ours. They lived in a big two-story white house with a wide porch in front and above it an upper porch, which we called a "portico."

The family consisted of a deaf-and-dumb son Alex, a daughter Sally, often referred to as an old maid though she later married and had several children, and twin boys, Paul and Dow, who were about the age of George. Another son, "Jeems Henry," younger than Alex, was married and lived in a "rent-house" some distance from the Taylor home and farmed some of his father's land.

My brother Tom and his wife, Lucy, could hardly be considered as neighbors, but Lucy's parents, Mr. and Mrs. McCarty, lived on their large farm joining Tom's place on the east. With them lived their son-in-law, Will Chaney, and his wife, Leona, Lucy's older sister. The Chaneys had no children, but the Mc-Cartys' grandson, Cam, lived with them. His father, George McCarty, was Lucy's older brother, whose wife had died soon after Cam was born. Jim McCarty, another brother, who lived directly south of us, eventually sold his farm to the Ponder family, who had a grown son and four or five daughters, but we never came to know them very well. Another family nearby were the Bourlands, who owned a large farm. They belonged to my father's church—the Primitive, or Old School, Baptist Church, commonly called the Hardshell Baptist Church.

Until John and Mattie Briley and their children left that part
of Texas they were our closest friends. They came to Texas
from Tennessee and lived a year or so on a rented farm adjoining
the one that my father had rented on the prairie. About the time
Father moved his family to our new home in the Cross Timbers
the Brileys bought and occupied a farm about three miles northeast of us. It was deeper in the woods than was ours but had a
fairly good house, outbuildings, fenced fields, and an orchard.

We visited the Brileys often and they often came to see us.
These visits were usually on Sunday, and when we spent the
entire day together. They had three sons and a daughter. The
older boys were Walter, a couple of years younger than George,
and Oscar, almost exactly my age. They were good kids and
would sometimes come over on Saturday afternoon and spend the
night and all day Sunday with us, or George and I would visit
them for a short weekend. We missed them a great deal when,
about 1890, Mr. Briley sold the farm and took his family to the
Prairie West.

In addition to our social contacts with the neighbors, we frequently had visitors who lived several miles away. One of our
perennial callers was Uncle Bill Lopp, who came to see us almost
once a week for ten years. He was a talkative old fellow, who
was reputed to have considerable knowledge of medicine.

One day, when I was about four years old, my sister Mattie
slipped out the back door and fled to the orchard when she saw
a mother and daughter coming whom she thoroughly disliked.
My mother gently reproved Mattie after the visitors had gone,
but the incident impressed me a great deal. As a result, the next
time I saw Mr. Lopp coming I hurried to the smokehouse in the

back yard and sat down in a corner behind a barrel of salt pork. Mother and George called me but I remained still as a mouse, fondly believing that the old man was being deprived of all the pleasure of his visit!! Not until by peeking through a crack I saw the old chap walking away smoking his pipe did I appear to face the family, somewhat flustered by my mysterious disappearance.

Although Mattie was a typical "teenager" of the time, she married when quite young, and therefore had only one beau who came to see her quite often while she lived in our Cross Timbers home. This was Benton Scott, a young telegraph operator of the Keller railroad station. As there were few social affairs for them to attend, Benton was more or less a "fireside companion" except for walks about the farm.

George discovered that by leaning a post up between the chimney and the outside wall of the kitchen it was possible for us to climb through the north window of the attic, where we slept. As soon as we had reached the attic George and I would pull dirt dauber's clay nests from the rafters, crumble them with our hands, and drop them through the cracks in the attic floor onto Benton's head when he was being entertained by Mattie in the living room below. She would grind her teeth with rage but was helpless. Aften Benton had gone she would urge Mother to give us both a licking, which of course we deserved, but our mother had such a keen sense of humor that she never did.

Since our house stood on a hill in plain sight of the railroad we were frequently visited by tramps. We always fed them but never let them come into the house. They were always asked to sit down on the little front porch and were given a generous meal of bread and butter, cold meat, preserves, and a quart can of milk or buttermilk. In cold weather my mother or Alice would sub-stitute a pot of coffee for the milk. Evidently the word got around among the hoboes that our home fed well, for hardly a week ever went by without our having a least one tramp as a visitor.

3. Vittles: Plain and Fancy

All the residents of the Cross Timbers demanded three square meals of what was collectively known as "vittles." These meals were always referred to as breakfast, dinner, and supper. Not until long after my boyhood days were past did I ever hear the midday meal called lunch or the evening meal dinner. In fact, the word "lunch" was hardly in the vocabulary of ourselves or most of the neighbors. A slice of buttered bread or some cheese and crackers eaten between meals was usually known as a "snack."

Breakfast did not differ much from the other two meals. Breakfast foods were unknown in our community. Biscuits, fried potatoes, bacon, eggs, butter, milk gravy sometimes called "hush-puppy gravy," and syrup or sorghum molasses constituted a good breakfast. Sometimes the thrifty housewife omitted the eggs, especially if the local grocery store was paying a good price for them. In the winter homemade sausage might take the place of bacon, and hominy and fried sweet potatoes were common. If "company" was present at breakfast, ham and eggs were often served and sometimes fried chicken.

In our home my father always said grace before every meal, unless we had one of his church brothers as a guest, in which case the guest was asked to "return thanks." In our household Father

saw to it that we were all present before grace was said and we
began eating. No doubt he would have been horrified by having
a child come drifting in when the rest of the family were half
through the meal.

As my father came to Texas from Nebraska and had spent
most of his life in Missouri, our fare was a bit different from that
of others in the community, who were either born and reared in
Texas or had come from the Deep South or Tennessee. Most
families from those states ate either cornbread or biscuits at every meal. My father said that he had eaten enough cornbread as
a Missouri farm boy to last him the rest of his life. Both my
mother and Alice made large snowy loaves of what was usually
called "light bread." Slices of this were often toasted on top of
the stove for breakfast, although biscuits made with buttermilk
and soda appeared more often on the breakfast table.

The striking difference between the food in this part of Texas
during the 1880's and that of today was that most of it was produced on the farm. Perhaps we raised more of our food than did
most of our neighbors because of the large orchard and garden,
and yet my father sometimes complained bitterly of the high cost
of living.

"When I was a boy in Missouri," he would often declare, "my
father had a big family and three or four Negro slaves, but a
hundred dollars in cash was all we spent in a year. Now I do not
have a big family at home but it takes two or three hundred
dollars a year to run us!" He would then explain that they tanned
their own leather, made their own shoes, and spun and wove the
wool from their sheep to make homespun clothing. He admitted,

however, that they ate cornbread three times a day every weekday and seldom had biscuits except on Sunday morning for breakfast.

Looking backward it seems to me now that we bought very little at the grocery store except sugar, coffee, flour, soda, syrup, salt, and pepper. We always bought green coffee, which was roasted in the oven and ground in a small coffee mill nailed to the wall above the cook-table. Very few persons drank tea, coffee being the universal beverage often served three times a day.

The grocery stores bought syrup in barrels and drew it into gallon jugs brought by customers. There were several types, such as sugar drip, ribbon cane, and corn syrup.

Nathan Vick, one of Mr. Taylor's renters, owned a sorghum mill and made sorghum every summer, not only from his own cane but "on the halves" for others in the community who grew sorghum cane and hauled it to the mill. A grist mill, which was a short distance east of Keller, ground corn, taking a share of the meal as "toll."

On the whole, the people of the Cross Timbers ate fairly well, though I felt that we fared a little better than most of our neighbors. During the summer there was little fresh meat since refrigerators were unknown and no ice was available to those living on farms. From time to time someone would kill a fat heifer and peddle out the beef, but as a rule chicken, fried, baked with dressing, or stewed with dumplings, was the nearest approach to fresh meat for a Sunday dinner. Ham, boiled or fried with "speckled gravy," was also quite suitable for any meal when company was present.

The word "meat" usually meant pork or bacon, sometimes called "side meat." Almost every family kept a few hogs. Father always butchered three or four every fall or early in the winter. For some days after "hog killing" we lived "high on the hog" with fried liver, baked spareribs, and boiled backbones.

Our father cut up the meat, trimming the hams, shoulders, and sides, which were "salted" down in a barrel or large box for a few weeks. After the pieces of meat had "taken salt" they were removed, the surplus salt was washed off, and the flesh side of the hams and shoulders were rubbed with brown sugar and pepper. They were then hung in the smokehouse and smoked by a small fire made with hickory or post-oak chips. The "side meat" might only have the surplus salt brushed off and kept as dry salt pork.

In common with our neighbors we always had a large garden planted with "Irish" potatoes, "English" peas, radishes, onions, "mustard greens," lettuce, cucumbers, beets, string beans, and squashes of various kinds. We also planted peanuts and a few rows of popcorn. Sweet-potato slips were grown in a bed and set out in rows to be dug in the fall. Turnips might be planted in early spring but more often in early fall as part of a "fall garden."

During the summer most families had plenty of green vegetables but in winter they often had only sweet potatoes, which were either kept in a cellar or heaped up on the ground and covered with a layer of straw, on top of which was spread a thick layer of earth so they would not freeze when cold weather came. Cabbage was seldom grown in our community but some families grew collards, but we never did; nor did we ever plant okra, which was a favorite vegetable of most of our neighbors who came from the Deep South.

One day George and I, while looking for wild grapes in the woods, found a "bee tree." It was a large hollow post-oak tree with numerous bees coming out or going into a hole about half-way up its trunk. We marked the tree by cutting a cross in the bark and a few days later our brother Tom helped cut it down. The hollow trunk burst open when it fell, revealing a large quantity of honey. Our father made a "bee hive" and Tom, who had half-a-dozen hives of bees and knew how to handle them, helped us to get them into the hive after they had attached themselves in a huge cluster to a branch of one of the nearby trees.

This started our bee keeping, but we later got three or more hives of bees. We "robbed" them about twice a year and so always had plenty of honey for our own use and some to give to our friends. It was put in stone or glass jars that were then placed on shelves in the cellar. Here were also put the large flat "crocks" of milk, as well as butter, pickles, jam, jelly, preserves, and canned fruit or anything else that should be kept cool. Sometimes a jug of buttermilk would be lowered by rope into the well, for although we could not drink the water it was quite cool!

Although there was a certain amount of sameness about the food of all the families in our community, no two housewives served their families meals that were exactly the same. The basic materials might be the same, but the blending and cooking brought differences. The McCarty's made salt-rising bread, which could be smelled by any visitor as soon as he entered the house.

Every woman made biscuits using the same ingredients, which were flour, buttermilk, lard, a little soda, and salt, but no two women's biscuits were alike. Some were large, tough, and of a bluish tinge; others light, dark brown, and flaky; some were streaked with soda, and others with too little soda were heavy and flat. They varied in size, too, but were usually of fairly generous proportions. All were made with sour milk and soda, for baking powder, sometimes referred to as "yeast powders," was considered not healthful, and the sour-dough biscuits of the Cow Country and Alaska were unknown in the Cross Timbers.

Dining rooms were virtually unknown by rural families. Everyone ate in the kitchen and there were no dining chairs. When visitors were present they sat in the living room until the hostess announced dinner. The host then asked everyone to bring his chair unless he happened to be sitting in a rocker. The straight chairs were of various types. Some had seats of rawhide, others of cane, and still others of wood. Along the wall behind the table in most homes was a long wooden bench, on which some of the children sat.

If several visitors were present there might not be room for the children at the table, so that they had to wait until their elders had eaten, which might seem a long time. Because screening was unknown one child would be given a leafy branch of a tree to wave back and forth above the table to keep flies away. Guests usually deplored this and urged that it was not necessary, for "everyone could mind his own flies."

Any youngster assigned to such a task fondly hoped that his parents would agree and relieve him of this tiresome duty. Having to wait was bad enough, but it was immeasurably worse when the child was in a situation where he could smell the food, see the choicest pieces of chicken disappear from the platter, and hear the shouts of the other kids, who were outside playing "black man" or "town ball."

When the summer was extremely hot my father would build a brush arbor just outside the back door of the kitchen. Beneath this he would put the dining table, the bench on which George and I sat at mealtime, and any chairs that were not needed in the house. It was far cooler to eat out there than in the kitchen that was heated by the big wood stove, on which the meal had been cooked. In case of rain the table would be brought back to the kitchen but it was taken outside again when the skies were clear.

Almost everyone in the community covered the table with an oilcloth except on Sunday or when company was present. Meat of some kind was served at almost every meal. In the summer the vegetables might be green beans boiled with a slab of salt pork, or mustard or turnip greens—again with salt pork. Green peas and new potatoes were boiled together and seasoned with butter and a little milk.

In winter navy beans were boiled with a ham hock or a piece of salt pork or bacon, or lima beans were boiled and seasoned with butter. Sweet potatoes, which were baked in the oven, were available in several varieties, but pumpkin yams were our favorite type.

In bitterly cold weather my father liked to roast sweet potatoes in the ashes of the fireplace in the living room. A dessert was seldom served on weekdays unless visitors were present but the molasses pitcher was on almost every table three times a day and virtually every meal was "topped off" by molasses.

One day when supper was a little late John Clark dropped by while we were eating. When asked to sit and eat with us he refused, saying that he had already "et" his supper. After a few minutes, however, he remarked, "I believe I will taste of them molasses." He picked up the pitcher and poured a little of its contents into a spoon, assumed a judicial attitude as he turned his head to one side, and finally said, "No, they're not quite like ours. Mighty good though."

Upon another occasion Lucy's nephew, Charlie Robinson, and his father, who was county assessor, stopped at our house about noon and were persuaded to sit down and have dinner with us. Charlie was slow of speech and still slower of action. After everyone else had finished Charlie continued eating until Mr. Robinson grew impatient to get back to his work.

"Come on Charlie," he said sharply. "You've eaten enough. Let's go!"

"Why Pappy," was the response, "I ain't tetched the molasses yet."

Although syrup was usually considered sufficient for an everyday meal, most families canned a considerable quantity of fruit, largely peaches and blackberries. It is a significant commentary, both on the size of the average family and the capacity of the youngsters for food, that almost every housewife bought half-gallon glass jars for canning instead of the quart or pint sizes commonly used today.

"Law no," one of our neighbor women once said to Alice, "I allus buy half-gallon jars cause a quart wouldn't go half-way 'round at our house."

Fruit jars cost so much that few families felt able to buy a sufficient number to serve canned peaches or berries except on Sunday or when "company" came. At other times, if any fruit ap-

peared on the table it was likely to be dried peaches or possibly dried apples. Because our orchard was large we had a great quantity of peaches to dry every summer. We also made a great deal of blackberry jam and peach preserves. In some instances these preserves were made with sorghum, which was far cheaper than sugar.

My father was more "forehanded" than were most of the neighbors. At hog-killing time we "rendered out" many stone jars of lard, and we always borrowed a big sausage mill and usually ground a washtub full of sausage. George always turned the mill, while my duty was to feed it with the meat Father had trimmed from the hams and shoulders, together with the tenderloins, putting in two strips of lean and one of fat.

After the meat was ground, it was seasoned with salt, black pepper, sage, and a little red pepper. Two or three sausage cakes were then fried and eaten in order to determine whether it was properly seasoned or needed a bit more salt, pepper, or sage. Once it had been approved, it was packed tightly in long cloth bags about three inches in diameter and hung in the smokehouse.

Sometimes part of it might be packed in gallon jars of stoneware, with melted lard poured on it to a depth of a couple of inches. These jars were then put in the cellar along with the stone jars of lard, honey, preserves, pickles, jelly, and jam, and glass jars of canned fruit. A jar or two of headcheese, sometimes called "souse," was made and placed in the cool cellar.

With these resources produced on the farm plus an ample supply of milk, buttermilk, eggs, butter, sweet potatoes, peanuts, and dried peaches, perhaps my father was justified in feeling sorry for any family that "lived out of paper sacks." It is doubtful if there were any of these in our part of the Cross Timbers but most of the wheat farmers on the nearby prairie might be so classified.

Although our daily fare throughout the week was plain and sometimes lacked variety, it was substantial, nourishing food calculated to "stick to the ribs" for several hours of hard work or active exercise. Almost without exception, the same was true of our neighbors. Most of them would have viewed with horror what is now called a "Continental breakfast," consisting of a sweet roll and coffee. A man who was to split rails, chop cotton, or plow from around sunrise until noon wanted meat, eggs, hot biscuits, gravy, and maybe pancakes!

Getting the children to eat is today a problem for many parents. This was not so in the Texas Cross Timbers in my boyhood days. Then the problem, if any, was to fill them up. The kids seemed perpetually hungry. Even getting them up for breakfast was no chore when they were awakened to smell the savory, sagey odor of frying sausage or of country-cured ham, and knew that eggs, hot biscuits, and plenty of butter and syrup or peach preserves would also be on the table.

If the weekday meals were substantial but plain, the "vittles" served at Sunday dinner or to any expected visitors were of such nature that they might be called "fancy." Because of the lack of refrigeration the type of food served to "company" depended to a considerable extent upon the season of the year. In the summer the meal was likely to include a big platter of fried chicken with a large bowl of cream gravy, green peas cooked with new potatoes, mustard greens, radishes, onions, and perhaps other vegetables from the garden. Dessert would be cake, custard or peach pie, or blackberry or peach cobbler.

In the winter the meal might consist of either boiled or baked ham or baked chicken with dressing, candied sweet potatoes, cabbage or turnips, lima beans, pickles, and the usual dessert of a fruit cobbler, pie, cake, preserves, and jelly. Chicken and dumplings might be served at any season and always there was butter, strong coffee, milk, and buttermilk. In the late fall or early winter the meat at a dinner for company might be baked spareribs or roast pork.

While a white or red tablecloth was spread over the weekday

oilcloth, I cannot recall having seen napkins on a table more than two or three times in ten years. They were of cloth, for if paper napkins had been made before the last decade of the nineteenth century they had not reached the Cross Timbers. The dishes in our home were ironstone china made by Meakin in Hanley, England, while Tom and Lucy's were Meakin lusterware, now eagerly sought by collectors willing to pay a high price for a lusterware plate or platter.

The children were usually taught "table manners" with great care by their parents, who diligently sought to "practice what they preached." It must be admitted, however, that some of these elders were at best a bit old-fashioned in their eating practices. Hot coffee would be "saucered and blowed" by some of the oldsters, and more than a few senior citizens who visited us used a table knife not only for cutting but as a "common carrier," just as did the writer of this old-time verse:

> I eat my beans with honey
> I've done it all my life
> They do taste kind of funny
> But it sticks them on the knife.

Such a person, however, thoughtfully put the coffee cup on his plate while he drank from the saucer in order to avoid staining the tablecloth and was careful to wipe or lick his knife clean before reaching for the butter!

Looking backward over three-quarters of a century, I feel that the vittles of the Cross Timbers dwellers were often more palatable than the food served today in many swank restaurants, where it costs a dollar or so to sit down and a great deal more to get up.

4. Reading: Common and Preferred

From the time we had stayed with Mrs. Blodgett, I began to feel that George and I were not quite like the other boys of the neighborhood. This did not mean a feeling that we were better or worse than the other kids of the community but only that we were *different*. Just how or why we were different never occurred to us, but it seems clear to me now that because we both read a great deal we lived, to some extent, in a make-believe world, into which few of our boyhood friends could enter.

Just when I learned to read with some degree of fluency would be hard to say, but it must have been by the time I was five or six years old or possibly even earlier. At any rate, when I entered school at the age of eight the teacher put me in the fourth-reader class and in a few weeks advanced me to the fifth-reader group.

My father read almost nothing except the Bible and his church paper, *The Signs of the Times,* devoted to the Old School Baptist cause and published in New York by Gilbert Bebee. Father knew the Bible almost from cover to cover, however, quoted passages from it constantly, and applied it to daily life.

There were not many books in our home except George's school books and mine, after I started to school. We also had a copy of *Pilgrim's Progress* with illustrations. This was most interesting to me and I must have read it at a very early age, for the allegory did not penetrate my skull. To me the giants Pope and Pagan as well as Giant Despair were real giants; Doubting Castle, the Slough of Despond, and the Key called "Promise" were only the names of a swamp, a castle, and a key.

My brother Henry had left us a copy of Longfellow's *Poems,* some neighbor had been kind enough to lend us a copy of "The Ancient Mariner" with illustrations by Doré, and another had given us a paperback thriller called *The Trader Spy.* There were a few others—a thick one-volume *History of the United States* and a copy of Sir Walter Scott's *Poems,* including his plays.

I also remember seeing, when very small, a novel entitled *The Eye That Never Sleeps,* and another, *Broken Links and Southern Soldiers.* Both of these and *The Trader Spy* must have been either temporary loans to Mattie or the property of one of the men my father hired from time to time to help pick cotton, for they had disappeared before I was able to read with any degree of fluency.

All the other books I read and reread many times, and I memorized many of the shorter poems of Longfellow and long passages of most of Scott's poems, including "Lay of the Last Minstrel," "Marmion," "Lady of the Lake," "Lord of the Isles," and at least a little of "Rokeby," "Bridal of Triermain," and "Harold the Dauntless." In addition, I memorized most of "The Ancient Mariner" and many of the poems in McGuffey's fourth and fifth readers. In fact, I memorized some from the sixth reader, for although I never studied it in school my brother John had given me a copy, and memorizing verse was always easy for me.

For some years the only periodical which we received except

my father's *Signs of the Times* was the semimonthly publication *The Farm and Fireside,* published by Mast, Crowell, and Kirkpatrick. As the name indicates, its contents consisted chiefly of articles on farm problems and household matters, including recipes, with usually one short story or an installment of a serial story.

Because of the scarcity of reading matter George and I always looked forward to the coming of every issue and read everything it contained, including the recipes and advertisements. If the magazine happened to be running a serial, or what we called a "continued story," we talked about it for days and each of us expressed his opinion of how it would end.

In reading the ads in the latest number of *The Farm and Fireside* we found a long list of books, any three of which could be had postpaid for a new two-year subscription or a renewal for two years by one already a subscriber. As the little journal cost only fifty cents a year this seemed such a bargain that we raked up a dollar and sent it in, naming the three books which we had selected.

Alice had chosen a cookbook, as she, like virtually all of the neighbor women, had never owned one but cooked largely "by ear." George selected *The Swiss Family Robinson,* and I, *Dick Onslow among the Indians.* When the books at last came George and I eagerly plunged into reading our selections, while Alice began the study of her cookbook and soon tried some of the most alluring recipes.

My own volume had a strong, spicy odor that was not too agreeable. This was probably because it had been stored in a room or box liberally treated with some insect repellent but as neither of the other two books had this scent I assumed that it was the smell of Indians!

Certainly, there were plenty of Indians in the story, which was a real thriller-diller, in which Dick and his buddy were both wounded in an Indian attack on a California-bound wagon train. The Indians were defeated but the two wounded men were inadvertently left behind when the wagon train resumed its journey. Their adventures during the next few weeks were amazing!

When each of us had finished his own book George and I exchanged volumes and for some weeks I lived with *The Swiss Family Robinson.* Interesting as were the adventures of Dick Onslow, those of Fritz, Ernest, James, Francis, and their parents were far more so. In our work and play we talked of them as though they were our close friends.

Even the animals of the Swiss family made some contribution to our daily lives. When our faithful old dog, Ring, died of old age and a neighbor gave us a pup we promptly named him "Turk" for the Swiss family's dog. Our old mother cat, originally called "Old Puss," we had named "Madame Arles" for the chief character in a short story that we had read. When she presented us with a batch of kittens, however, we named one "Nip" for the Swiss family's monkey; another, "Bruin," Dick Onslow's designation of a bear; and a third, "Fedora," again from a short story.

When *The Farm and Fireside* announced that a quart glass fruit jar had been filled with corn and that a prize of one hundred dollars would be paid to the subscriber who could guess the closest to the number of grains it contained, George and I were much excited. We quickly borrowed an empty quart fruit jar from Alice, filled it with shelled corn, and carefully counted the number of grains it held. The publishers had set the date when the jar would be opened, the grains counted, and the winner of the award announced in the columns of the magazine.

The number our jar had contained was something over 1,800. George had carefully jotted down the date when the official count was to be made and when at last the day came, gave a monologue with only Alice and me as an audience.

"Well, I guess they're counting right now. Probably old Mast is saying, 'I've got 621 grains. How many do you have Crowell? You say 593? How about you, Kirkpatrick? 637? All right we'll add 'em up. It looks like that feller Dale down at Keller, Texas, has hit it almost exactly and will be the winner'."

It is always fun to dream, but the official count was over 2,600 grains instead of the some 1,850 which our quart jar held! Evidently a grain of corn, like everything else in Texas, grows big!

While we continued to read *The Farm and Fireside,* we eventually subscribed to the St. Louis *Republic,* which as I recall was at first a weekly and later a semiweekly newspaper. This gave us more to read, but both George and I eagerly sought books and magazines or any other reading matter. There was no opportunity for selection because very few families in the community read much. As a result, we read what we could get, regardless of whether it was trash or a classic.

Somewhere we acquired a copy of H. Rider Haggard's *King Solomon's Mines,* which we read and reread with much pleasure. While it never could hold a place in our affections equal to that of the *Swiss Family Robinson,* we talked about it a great deal and even tried to play the story, using part of the south field as the desert, and the corn crib as the mountains, while each of us assumed the role of two or three of the principal characters in the story.

The Taylor twins, Paul and Dow, and their sister, Miss Sally, were apparently the only other persons in our neighborhood who read much except ourselves and our brother Tom. One day when Father had gone to the Taylor home on an errand he returned with a huge pile of magazines, which Miss Sally had sent us.

This was a delightful surprise. Most of them were copies of a magazine called *Good News* devoted largely to fiction, including a number of serials. Fortunately, the file was unbroken and each "continued story" was equivalent to a book. Some of these were "Breakneck Farm or the Merriman Twins," "Boys Will Be Boys or a Harvest of Wild Oats," "Peter Potter the Page," and a sequel, "Peter Potter's Pilgrimage or the Lively Vice Consul to Korea."

Just why authors of that time should give double-barrel titles to their books is a deep dark mystery. Possibly they could not make up their minds as to which title was better, or, more likely, the practice was designed to attract the hoped-for reader's interest. Neither George nor I were concerned about this. It was enough to know that we had some rattling good yarns to read, for which we were most grateful.

Until after 1887 I had never been more than six or seven miles from home except once when Lucy and Alice took me to Fort Worth by train to spend part of a day with Lucy's sister. In the autumn of that year my sister Fannie, and her husband, Mace Hutchinson, and their two children came down from Nebraska to spend the winter with us.

About this time my brother Henry and Mattie's husband, Herbert Acers, established a general-merchandise store at the little town of Navajoe in Greer County. This village was about forty-five miles north of Vernon, Texas, and only about three miles from the North Fork of the Red River. Beyond this stream lay the great Kiowa-Comanche Indian Reservation.

The two partners in the firm of Acers and Dale hoped to sell much merchandise to the Indians, as well as to the ranchmen who leased their lands, and to sell supplies to the foremen of trail herds on the Western Trail from Texas to Dodge City, which was only three or four miles west of the little town. A few settlers were also coming in to establish homes in the area between the north and south forks of Red River and extending west to the hundredth meridian, which Texas had organized as Greer County in 1860 under the assumption that the North Fork was the main stream. This was denied by officials of the United States, who claimed that the South Fork was the principal stream and should be considered the Red River.

When Mattie learned that Fannie and her family were visiting us, she wrote urging all of us to come to visit Henry and her. Fannie and Alice thought it too much of a trip to make in the winter but Father and Mace went by train to Vernon, where they were met and taken to Navajoe. After a stay of two weeks they returned, praising with enthusiasm the beauties of this part of Greer County.

As spring approached, the Hutchinsons returned to Nebraska but Father continued to talk about Navajoe and Greer County. A born pioneer, he was always eager to go to a new land. When Jay wrote that he had resigned his job in Mexico and settled on a claim half a mile south of Navajoe, Father decided to rent the farm for a year and spend the winter in Greer County.

We all approved of this wholeheartedly. It was now around the first of September and the cotton must be picked, the corn gathered, and livestock disposed of before we could all leave. It was therefore decided that Alice and I should go by train to Vernon, where someone would meet us, and Father and George should stay until the crops were harvested, and then come out by wagon.

Alice and I left late in October. The trip was most interesting to a nine-year-old kid who had never been on a train but once before, and then only to make the round trip from Keller to Fort Worth. The Fort-Worth-and-Denver train on which we traveled was slow, but it seemed to be moving at dizzying speeds and the day coach with red plush seats was to me most luxurious. When we saw our first prairie dogs I was certain that we had reached the real West.

When we arrived in Vernon at about 4:30 P.M., we were met by Jay with a wagon and team to take us to Navajoe, forty-five miles to the north. We camped on the prairie the first night and reached our destination late the following day. Mattie, Herbert, and Henry all seemed delighted to see us. The Acers-and-Dale store seemed to me very big. Mattie and Herbert and their baby daughter lived in an apartment attached to the north side of the store. Henry boarded with them but slept on a cot in the store in the part partitioned off in one corner for the Post Office, as he was postmaster.

Alice stayed with Mattie until Father and George came about the latter part of November, but I "bached" with Jay, who had

built a half dugout on his claim half a mile southwest of the
Navajoe townsite. We were quite comfortable, for although half-
way underground Jay's little place had a wood floor and a half
window on either side. It was furnished with two beds, a couple
of chairs, a small cookstove, a table, and a cupboard containing
dishes and cooking utensils.

Jay was building sheds for his horses, fencing a pasture, and
otherwise improving his claim. This was done in leisurely fashion
and I helped as much as possible. Every evening after supper Jay
would slip his forty-five Colt's revolver inside the waistband of
his trousers and go "to get the mail," though I cannot recall that
we ever got any mail. Jay would usually sit on the counter and
visit with other men, while I would usually go in and talk with
Mattie and Alice or read, for to my delight Mattie had a great
deal of wonderful reading matter.

As the arrival of Father and George created a housing problem, a large dugout room was quickly built joining Jay's half
dugout, and a door was cut connecting the two rooms. Alice then
came to keep house for Father, Jay, and George, while I replaced
her in Mattie's home. The new dugout was finished none too
soon, for about this time my brother John came in from North
Dakota, where he had remained working as a cowhand when Jay
left for the job in Mexico.

Probably I would have preferred staying on the claim in order
to spend more time with George, but it was fun to live with Mattie too. She was a subscriber to the *Youth's Companion* and had
many back numbers, which I read with much pleasure. In addition, she had a number of books which were most interesting.
Among them were *Surry of Eagle's Nest* and a sequel to it called

Mohun, both by John Esten Cooke. They were Civil War stories dealing with the campaigns of Stonewall Jackson and J.E.B. Stuart. I "ate them up" and from them learned a great deal.

Unfortunately, not all of Mattie's books and magazines were of the caliber of these two or the *Youth's Companion.* Many of them, such as *The Trappers of Arkansas* and the saccharine effusions of Charlotte M. Braeme and Mary Cecil Hay, were sheer trash, but I read them all. Many were published by the F. M. Lupton Company and sold for a few cents each, including such titles as *Lord Lisle's Daughter, Reaping the Whirlwind, A Mad Passion, Thrown on the World,* and a host of others. Because one volume, which I found very interesting, lacked the covers and title page it was impossible to know the name of either the author or the book. Many years later I learned that it was Victor Hugo's *Toilers of the Sea.*

When I moved to Mattie's home Father decided that it was best for me to attend the Navajoe school, which began early in November. The school house, made of boxing planks, was in the northwest part of town. The children sat on long wooden benches, while a wood-burning stove supplied heat. There were about thirty-five pupils ranging in age from six to seventeen years.

The teacher, Miss Anna Davidson, was a maiden lady of uncertain age, who lived with her widowed mother in the southwest part of the little town. She had an excellent library as judged by the standards of the region. Among her books were most of the novels of Dickens, Scott, and John Strange Winter, the poems and some prose works of Bulwer-Lytton, and books by George Eliot, Hawthorne, Cooper, and various others.

She soon learned that I liked to read and began to lend me books. As a result, during the winter and spring of 1888–1889 I read a number of Dickens' novels, including *David Copperfield, Pickwick Papers, Bleak House, Old Curiosity Shop,* and some others. Also, I read several of Scott's Waverly novels, George Eliot's *Mill on the Floss,* and several other books by various authors. Plenty of time was available in which to read, for my school studies were easy and I had little to do except for helping Mattie with the housework.

George remained in Greer County only about three months. As spring approached he received a letter from Tom offering to pay him eighty dollars to return and help him on the farm during the spring and summer months. As this seemed important money to a fifteen-year-old lad, George gladly accepted the offer.

Naturally I missed him a great deal, for we had never been separated except for the six weeks between my departure with Alice for Navajoe and his arrival with Father. During those weeks there had been so many interesting things for me to see that there was little time left in which to get lonesome. Now I began to get a little homesick for our Cross Timbers home and the kids that I had played with, but especially for George!

There was still much about life in the little town of Navajoe, however, to interest me. The Indians, wearing red blankets and beaded moccasins, with their hair in long braids tied with red yarn, especially fascinated me. Hardly a week went by without a few of them coming from the Reservation beyond the North Fork to pitch their tepees at the edge of town. Usually they would stay two or three days, coming to the stores to buy groceries, bright-colored calico, and other merchandise.

Few of them could speak much English, but Henry knew a little of the Comanche language. He taught me a few Comanche words and to count "in Comanche." This information I treasured carefully to spring on the neighbors' kids when we got back to our home in the Cross Timbers.

Early in May, 1889, Alice was married to Henry Roach, a young widower, who lived in Henrietta, Texas. I am not sure where she first met him but it was probably in Dallas when she was working in a hospital in that city. He was a contractor and builder, who also was an expert bricklayer and stonemason. He came to Navajoe for the wedding, but immediately took his bride to his home in Henrietta.

With George and Alice both gone, my father grew increasingly restless and early in June decided to return to the Cross Timbers. We could not regain possession of our home until the tenant had harvested his crops, which would be in November, but we could live with Tom and Lucy and help with the farm work. Probably the chief factor in Father's decision was his church. He missed the old friends and neighbors, but especially he missed his brethren in the Primitive Baptist Church, and the association with them in their homes and at worship.

At first he considered leaving me with Mattie for a few months but finally decided to take me with him. We left Navajoe early in June in a covered wagon drawn by a pony team. Our route was to Doan's Crossing on the South Fork of the Red River and to Vernon, Texas. From there we followed roads paralleling the Fort Worth and Denver Railway.

We reached Henrietta about ten o'clock one morning and stayed long enough to have noonday dinner with Alice and her husband. It was characteristic of my father, however, that soon after dinner we continued our journey. We were both pleased to note that Alice had an attractive home and seemed to be very happy.

We reached the western edge of the Upper Cross Timbers at Bowie and emerged from them near Aurora. Just ten days after leaving Navajoe we rolled up to the home of Tom and Lucy. Our ten-day trip would now be considered only a half-day's drive by car.

I was delighted to see George again and much pleased to see Tom and Lucy. It seemed that we had been away a long time and the familiar scenes of the Cross Timbers neighborhood looked very good to me after an absence of some eight months. While we could not occupy our own home until the old renter, Mr. Pulliam, and his two daughters, commonly called "Adar" and "Idar," had harvested their crops, it would be fun to live with Tom and Lucy for a time.

The few months of life in the Prairie West had stimulated my imagination. I had seen real cowboys and Indians, had lived for several weeks in a half dugout, and had often climbed the Navajoe Mountains, only a mile east of the little town named for them.

Of course, after we had returned to our Cross Timbers home I was not slow in telling my boy friends of these experiences and adventures with enough details and embellishments to make my stories interesting. When asked about Indians, I assured my questioner that they often camped near town and came to my brother Henry's store wearing blankets and moccasins, with their hair in two long black braids, and their faces painted.

Yes, I had seen the great Comanche Chief Quanah Parker many times. My brother Henry had traded with the Comanches so much that he knew their language fairly well and he had taught me some words and how to count in the Comanche tongue. When my bug-eyed listeners demanded a demonstration, I began, "sem-us, wo-hot, pie-heet, ah-tery-o-quit, mah-vit, nah-vit, tie-suit, nem-o-wah-sute, wo-ma-nie, say-men." This is one to ten.

While this boosted my stock a bit among my Cross Timbers playmates, by far the most important result of my western trip was that I had read a great deal more than I would have had the opportunity to do if we had spent the winter on the Cross Timbers farm. Some of it was trash but the major part was good literature, which, even as a boy, I preferred to read when given a choice. Reading greatly affected both my work and play, not only in my boyhood days but throughout my life.

5. "Six Days Shalt Thou Labor"

John Clark once remarked that "Heaven will be jus' lak it is here 'ceptin we won't hafta work." If John was correct in his conception of Paradise there were a few men in our Cross Timbers community who were enjoying Heaven here on earth! Not so my father. He had little patience with loafers and wondered how they were able to live in idleness. Yet, I heard him say once that it seemed sometimes that there was not more than fifty cents difference between the man who worked and the man who didn't, and that the one who *didn't* got the fifty cents!

This was obviously only a joke, for up to the time of his final illness his amazing energy was noted by all who knew him. Even at the age of sixty-five he could do more work in a day than any of his seven sons. Not only did he work hard himself but he demanded that his children do the same. Summer or winter he was up at dawn and calling George and me before he started to the barn to milk our three or four cows. Winter mornings in our attic bedroom was like the Arctic Circle; we would count "one, two, three," at which point we would toss back the covers and hit the icy floor with our bare feet. Dressing was quickly done, for we slept in our underwear. In two or three minutes we were clothed and standing before the fire downstairs, for Father always lighted fires in both the fireplace and kitchen stove before going to milk the cows.

Just when I started to do useful work and ceased to be a total liability is impossible to say, but it must have been at a very early age. Yet I cannot recall doing much before my mother's death except help pile brush when Father was clearing land. Also, of course, I had such chores as gathering up the eggs, bringing in chips or corn cobs for the kitchen stove, running errands, and pulling up weeds in the garden.

After my sister Alice became our housekeeper, however, I gradually began to do more to help in the household work and to do some work in the fields. My father encouraged and taught me to do farm work. He had grown up in an era when a farmer raised his own help, just as he raised his own fruit, vegetables, and·meat. Four or five husky sons, if properly taught, were a distinct asset. Otherwise it would not have been possible to feed and clothe a family of ten or twelve, which was not considered unusually large seventy-five years ago.

Even as a very little youngster I realized that carving a farm out of even a small tract of timberland required an enormous amount of hard work. Many times, when I was only four or five years old, my father would take me with him when he went to work in the woods. To me it was most interesting to watch him cut down the big post-oak trees and trim off the branches. It was also fun to watch him split a log into rails. For this he used a maul, which he made of hardwood, and an iron wedge to start a split of the log. Once a crack had been opened he used two or three hardwood wedges called "gluts" to widen it and at last split the log wide open. The two halves were then further divided by the same process into rails.

Even at that early age I could help a bit by piling brush or taking Father a drink of water. Our large peach orchard usually furnished us with far more fruit than we could use. Father had a light spring wagon commonly called a "hack." He would load this with peaches about wheat-harvest time and peddle them out among the wheat farmers on the prairie, who seldom tried to raise fruit of any kind on their black, waxy land. Their wives needed fruit very much at harvest time because threshing grain, and sometimes even cutting and shocking it, was a cooperative enterprise. This meant that a threshing crew of a dozen or more hungry men had to be fed and every housewife sought to outdo all the neighbor women in feeding them.

Wheat harvest, however, seldom lasted over three or four weeks at most; moreover, many of our peach trees were seedlings that produced the small freestone type of fruit that was hard to sell and therefore had to be dried. For weeks almost every summer "all hands and the cook" worked at cutting peaches in half, tossing the seeds aside, and setting out the peach halves with the cut side up on any flat surface to dry in the sun. Since, obviously, even a small child can cut a peach in half and put it out to dry, I very early put in weeks every summer helping to dry peaches. We also had about a quarter of an acre in blackberries, and picking blackberries was part of the work for George and me to do every summer.

When Alice became our housekeeper, I helped quite a bit in the house by washing and drying dishes, doing the churning, and bringing in wood and kindling.

One day George and I were in the orchard when peaches were ripe and we saw a woman and a little girl in a buggy drive up to our yard gate and go in the house. Neither of us knew them but presently I heard Alice calling me. George grinned as he said, "I'll bet she wants you to bring that little girl out to the orchard and get her some peaches."

I was sure that Alice wanted me to bring in some wood so I leaned back and stuck my chest out, answering, "Not *me*. If she asks me to do *that* I'll tell her to let th' little dickens go and get peaches for *herself* if she wants 'em. I'm not waitin' on any baby girl like her."

When Alice called again I yelled "Comin'" and started for the house in a lope, secure in my certainty that she wanted some wood.

"Ed," said Alice as I came in, "take this little girl out to the orchard and get her some peaches."

I swallowed a couple of times and replied, "Yes Ma'am!" Thinking back over three-quarters of a century to this little incident it seems plain what sort of kid I was, but I am hopeful that the child is not *always* "father to the man."

Our equipment for farming consisted of one breaking plow, a "Georgia stock" commonly called a "bull tongue" plow, a double shovel used to cultivate crops, a big farm wagon, the hack which Father used to peddle fruit and sweet potatoes, and that was about all. In addition, we had an axe, rake, pitchfork, two or three hoes, a grubbing hoe called a "mattock," a crosscut saw, handsaw, hatchet, and claw hammer. It is doubtful if all the farming implements and tools cost much over $150.00 when new.

Power was supplied by a small sorrel horse named Pompey, a

little bay mare called Net, and a larger, older mare known as Old Nell. All three of these animals could not have been sold for a total of $75.00, including the harness and old saddle. Old Nell died, apparently of old age, before we made our visit to Greer County. While out there Father sold Net and bought from an Indian for $14.00 a little yellow mare, that George and I promptly dubbed "Comanch." She was a typical Indian pony with an evil temper which was probably due to being teased by some papoose, for she bit my arm the first time I sought to put a bridle on her. As compared with the agricultural machinery most farmers have today, our equipment seems most meager and primitive. One modern tractor alone would cost two or three times as much as all my father's farm implements, tools, and horses were worth.

Even before our western venture I had done a great deal of work in the field chopping cotton, thinning corn, and cutting sprouts that sprang up in any newly cleared field. Like most children in the South, I had also done a great deal of cotton picking; therefore, by the time Father and I returned from the Prairie West late in June, 1889, I was fairly experienced in both field work and household duties, including a little cooking.

It was a joy to be back in the Cross Timbers neighborhood again, although we could not move into our own home until Mr. Pulliam had harvested his scanty crops. We lived with Tom and Lucy for some six weeks in order to assist Tom, who needed help in getting his crops "laid by," which, in the lingo of the South, meant the final plowing and hoeing of the corn and cotton. Then John Briley, who was moving to Roanoke to operate a small meat market, asked us to occupy his house and care for his cows and pigs until he could sell them, and the man to whom he rented his farm could move in. This we were glad to do and "bached" in his home for a month.

By that time the cotton-picking season had come, and we returned to Tom's home to help him with the first picking of his cotton crop. There would be a second picking when the rest of the bolls had opened, but that would be a month later. Until then there seemed comparatively little to do on Tom's farm. If we had been in our own home Father would have found plenty of work for all three of us clearing land, building or repairing fences, and doing any other thing needed to improve the farm.

Unwilling to remain idle, he decided that we should drive west to Parker County in the Upper Cross Timbers, where we had heard that there was a great demand for hands to pick cotton and gather corn. We accordingly packed the wagon with the necessary food and bedding, put on the bows and canvas cover, and headed west. After crossing the wide belt of prairie we entered the Upper Cross Timbers and on the second evening camped in a grove of trees on the banks of Walnut Creek.

We were on land belonging to Mr. McCrory, who grew corn, cotton, sorghum cane, and other types of feed on his farm of four or five hundred acres. He was in sore need of cotton pickers and help to gather corn, which in most Southern states is not husked but snapped from the stalks in the husk or "shuck." He paid seventy-five cents a hundred for cotton picking and three cents a bushel for gathering corn.

Unfortunately, it had been raining and the cotton and corn were both wet. We spent the next day or two in fixing up our camp while we waited for sunshine to dry them so that we could work. We were camped at the edge of a field of millet which had been cut and shocked. Just beyond were shocks of sorghum.

Father cut down a sapling to make a ridgepole. One end of this was lashed to a tree and the other rested in the fork of another long pole sharpened with an axe and driven into the ground. Over this ridgepole was stretched the canvas wagon sheet to make a tent. Enough tall stalks of cane were brought to form a wall at the back and a thick layer of millet was spread on the ground beneath the canvas. In the back part of this shelter we spread our blankets and slept at night, while in the front we kept the food and cooking utensiles.

We lived in this crude camp for over a month while George and I picked cotton. George could pick from 250 to 300 pounds a day, while my limit was about 150 pounds. Father, who had never acquired any skill in picking cotton, gathered corn, which weighs about seventy-two pounds to the bushel in the husk. As he could gather a hundred bushes a day and was paid three cents a bushel, he made about as much money a day as George and I both did picking cotton at seventy-five cents a hundred.

Pickers were so hard to find that Mr. McCrory had only a young Mr. Daugherty and George and me as hired help. As a result, his whole family, consisting of a twenty-year-old son, a seventeen-year-old daughter named Cynthia, twelve-year-old Georgia, and a little girl of six called Dora, picked every day. Even his wife came out every afternoon and picked cotton until time to go home and cook supper.

Except when picking beside Cynthia, in whom he apparently

had a romantic interest, Mr. Daugherty sang most of the time. Unfortunately, he seemed to know only one song and just a single stanza of it:

> Jesse had a wife
> Who mourned all her life
> Three children they were brave
> But a dirty little coward
> Shot Mr. Howard
> And laid Jesse James in his grave.

After I heard this all day long it seemed to ring in my ears when I lay down to sleep at night.

When we had finished picking all of McCrory's cotton, we picked for a neighboring farmer, Mr. Chandler, who paid us a dollar a hundred for picking a field that had been covered with water when Walnut Creek overflowed its banks after a heavy rain.

We became acquainted with three or four other families living near our camp and found all of them "mighty clever people," the word *clever* meaning generous and kind in the vernacular of the Cross Timbers. When George and I called on the Nelsons to see if we could buy a gallon of sorghum and half a bushel of sweet potatoes they seemed glad to let us have them. They refused any payment, however, saying that they "*would* not dream of charging a neighbor for a jug of sorghum molasses and a few sweet potatoes." We were much pleased by their generosity, but applying the term "neighbor" to persons camping for a few weeks half a mile farther down the creek seemed to be stretching the word quite a bit at least.

This generous attitude seemed to be typical of everyone we

met during our stay in the Walnut Creek camp. Mr. Chandler brought us a big piece of beef cut from half of a quarter that he had bought from someone who had butchered a fat heifer and was peddling out the meat to families in the community. Father did most of the cooking over a camp fire built in front of our so-called tent. Biscuits were baked in a Dutch oven, while beans were boiled in an iron pot with a slab of salt pork to season them. We often had hot cakes for breakfast, with bacon, sorghum, and dried fruit, plus plenty of hot coffee; all of us gained weight.

When, after a few weeks, most of the cotton had been picked Father decided it was about time to return home. We all felt that it had been a successful venture. Unfortunately, there had been several days when rain or misty weather made it impossible to pick cotton or gather corn. At such times George and I had fished or hunted, unless it was actually raining. Yet, on every working day we had made five or six dollars. Because our living had cost very little, by the time we started home we had saved seventy or eighty dollars. This was important money at a time when bacon sold for nine or ten cents a pound, and a good farm hand could be hired for fifteen dollars a month, plus board.

Once we were back at Tom's place we helped him pick the rest of his cotton. By that time our tenant, Mr. Pulliam, had finished harvesting his crop and had rented another small farm. To this he and his daughters, Adar and Idar removed, and we occupied our old home once more after an absence of nearly a year.

We were all most happy to be back home, and the neighbors seemed pleased also. In "neighborly fashion" they told us that the shiftless Mr. Pulliam had allowed most of the blackberries and peaches to ripen and fall to the ground and rot. Plainly, he had not kept up the fences or barn and sheds and he had allowed the weeds and sprouts to grow up in the fields.

With characteristic energy our father set to work with the help of George and me to put the little farm and its improvements in good order again. He bought two or three milk cows, a couple of sows with their litters of pigs, and a dozen or more hens. The fences were mended, the fields plowed, the fruit trees checked for borers, and the orchard enlarged by our setting out forty or fifty more peach trees.

During my stay with Mattie in Greer County I had done a bit of the cooking. This now helped, for we were keeping "bachelor's hall" and had to do all of our own housework, including preparing our own meals. So-called mixes, and biscuits and rolls ready to pop into the oven, which have saved the reason of many young brides and the lives of their husbands, lay several decades in the future. In consequence, we had to deal with the raw materials in our culinary efforts.

Father, whose experience went back to the days of the California gold rush, did most of the cooking, but I could do a fair job at "skillet slinging" myself, even if only ten years old. As George was a fair housekeeper we got along in excellent fashion and even entertained a good many persons at dinner or for overnight, including old Mr. Lopp and some of my father's brethren in the Primitive Baptist Church.

Toward spring Lucy, who was a remarkably good cook but a notoriously sloppy housekeeper, sponsored a surprise party for us. She conspired with seven or eight other women of the neighborhood to bring food for a sumptuous dinner and come to our bachelor home soon after breakfast to clean every inch of the house and prepare the noonday feast. They came in full force, each bringing her contribution of food.

After looking the situation over, with two or three suggesting that maybe they should go home and clean up their *own* houses, they set to work. Some prepared the dinner, while others washed the windows and did a bit of scrubbing. Then, after finding a large stack of copies of the St. Louis *Republic,* they decided to paper the living room and small "side room" with newspapers. Because we did not have enough copies of *The Republic* to complete the project, one lady sent her son home to bring back an armload of another newspaper, to which she and her husband subscribed.

It was a grand day, for two or three women had brought their children, and we had a lot of fun playing "hide-and-seek" and marbles while their mothers cooked and mixed flour-and-water paste, and applied it to the newspapers with which they covered the rough walls. Although it was to be a surprise party, I am sure that someone must have given Father a tip as to what had been planned. It is true that he *seemed* surprised but rather overdid it. Everyone had a good time but, unfortunately for me, these amateur paper hangers pasted some papers upside down or "slaunch-wise" on the walls. This almost forced me to stand on my head or in a slanting position to read them!

With the coming of warm weather we were kept very busy planting corn and cotton, setting out sweet-potato slips, and making a garden. We even planted a patch of peanuts and a few rows of popcorn. Father and George did most of the plowing, but in thinning corn or chopping cotton and other work done with a hoe George and I worked together. From the time I was

four or five years old and had been told such stories as "Jack and
the Beanstalk," "Cinderella," "Little Red Ridinghood," and
"Sinbad the Sailor," George and I had told one another stories
which we had "made up" ourselves. They usually began, "Once
you and I were little fairies."

Now that we were older and had read a good deal we resumed
this practice to relieve the tedium of working all day in the field
at such mechanical tasks as thinning corn and chopping or picking cotton. After reading the *Swiss Family Robinson* our stories
ran largely to being shipwrecked on some desert island. Sometimes we were accompanied by two of our playmates, Walter and
Oscar Briley. With complete disregard for geography the wreck
usually occurred while we were on a voyage across the Atlantic
to enter school in England.

Not all of our made-up tales were based on wrecks while at
sea and attacks by pirates or savages. Some of them were "West-
erns," probably due to our reading *Dick Onslow among the Indians* or *The Trader Spy*. In these we were usually on our way
to California with a wagon train and had been captured by Indians when we left it for an hour or so of hunting. After reading
a book about Africa, which the Taylors had been kind enough
to lend us, our yarns tended to shift to the Dark Continent. They
usually dealt with lion hunts and adventures with Pygmies.

Our story telling was to sustain an enormous advance from an
unexpected source the following year. We made a good crop of
corn and cotton in 1890, and the peach trees were loaded with
fruit. As a result, we worked hard drying peaches all summer and
harvesting the field crops during the autumn months. The wheat
crop of the prairie farmers was also good, and Father was able to

sell all the blackberries and best peaches at what was then considered a good price.

In February, 1891, my brother John wrote that he had just married and settled on a claim, where he had built for his bride a large and comfortable sod house. There was little prospect of making a crop on freshly plowed sod, however, and if Father could rent some additional land he and his wife would be glad to come down and make a crop with us. Father accordingly rented a twenty-acre field about three-quarters of a mile southeast of us to be planted in cotton. The terms were for the renter to receive three-fourths and the landowner one-fourth of the money derived from the sale of the crop.

This twenty-acre field was level, fertile land which had formerly had a house on it occupied by a family named Moore. The house had either burned or been moved but the tract of land was still known as the "Moore farm." In the corner where the house had stood was a small plot of grass and a big apple tree that bore large, long apples resembling the variety called "sheep's nose." Evidently the tree was a seedling, for the fruit was extremely sour and never seemed to ripen.

Once this field had been rented, Father wrote to John, who, with his wife, Ava, arrived by train late in February. We were all delighted to have them with us. Ava was only nineteen years old, while John was about twenty-seven. She was a gay, lively girl, the oldest of a bevy of sisters ranging from seventeen to three or four years of age, though she had an older brother, who was married and lived in Dallas.

As the oldest of so many sisters, Ava had been forced to assume a measure of responsibility in her parents' household. She was an excellent cook and a remarkably good housekeeper. Her big snowy loaves of homemade bread, six-layer chocolate cakes, golden-brown doughnuts, and luscious pies were most welcome additions to our bachelor fare of the past year. To our great distress, a late freeze wiped out our crop of peaches, but we had berries and the products of a big garden.

A couple of months after John and Ava joined us, Ava's mother and a seven- or eight-year-old daughter, Minnie, came to see us. They had gone to Dallas to visit the son and family and were returning to their home in Vernon, Texas, with a stop-off to see Ava and the family into which she had married. We all liked Ava's mother, Mrs. Brown, very much. Apparently she largely supported her family by keeping boarders, while her husband, a more or less worthless old fellow, contributed a little by working at odd jobs that he could find.

Mrs. Brown stayed only a day or so but left Minnie with us for the summer, which pleased Ava and me very much. Minnie was a nice kid, and because I was two or three years older she came to regard me as the fountainhead of knowledge and wisdom. This was a new role for me, which I savored to the fullest. Hitherto I had been the one to seek knowledge from George by asking numerous questions, which he never failed to answer.

With John to help with the work, even the addition of twenty acres of cotton did not require my spending as much time in the field as usual. As a result, I helped Ava with the housework, with Minnie as my able assistant. I soon found that she liked stories and when we were working or playing alone she proved an enthusiastic audience for my made-up narratives, usually about nations of Pygmies about a foot tall. These little people often engaged in wars, in which a part of the troops rode into battle mounted on jack rabbits! Minnie even told some stories of her own, in which her only toy, a "sleepy doll" named Pearl, was always a leading character.

When the time came to chop cotton, I had to lend a hand part of the time. Knowing that our scholarly brother John had read many more books than we had, George asked him to tell us one of his favorite novels. John was willing but said that he would rather tell an original story. That suited us exactly; for the next few months he and George, when working in the field, took turns in relating some amazing narratives. I was not able to hear all of these, but new ones were started in the fall when we began picking cotton, which kept all three of us in the field all day.

The summer slipped by as if on fleet wings. When it became intensely hot our father built a brush arbor in the back yard. We moved the dining table out of the steaming hot kitchen and set it up under this shady arbor, which made eating our meals and the aftermath of washing the dishes far more comfortable. As we had no peaches to prepare for drying, we all had more leisure than in previous summers. Minnie was a good playmate as well as a good listener to my stories, and I was truly sorry when late in August two of her older sisters, who had been visiting in Dallas, came by with instructions from their mother to take her home.

Ava returned to Greer County in October, going to Vernon by train, where she was met by Henry. John stayed another month to finish picking the cotton crop. He then bought an old wagon

and a yoke of oxen, and drove to Navajoe. This must have given
Ava ample time to put their sod house in order, for travel by ox
team was indeed slow.

Some of the stories told by John and George were truly thrill-
ers, and following the pattern set by the imagination of John,
George and I continued to relate amazing narratives of adventures by land and sea as long as we lived in the Cross Timbers. I
recall one in which George was seeking gold in Alaska, when he
discovered a hidden valley with a warm climate due to many
large hot springs. Here the vegetation grew almost as rank as in
the tropics and a few mastodons were found.

In another yarn he had sought to reach the South Pole by
balloon. With a parachute strapped to his back and with chemi-
cals to generate enough gas to reinflate the balloon so that he
could return after a landing, he drifted south from Australia.
Upon reaching the Antarctic continent he floated over a range of
high mountains and discovered a valley with a subtropical climate caused by smouldering volcanoes. Here he was forced to
bail out because of a gas leak but, relieved of his weight, the
balloon rose enough to pass over the mountains to the south.

He landed safely, but soon after he had repacked the parachute and strapped it to his back he was seized by four tall black
warriors armed with spears. He tried to talk to them by signs,
but with little success. They led him to a village of round grass
houses, where black men, women, and children seemed much
excited by his appearance. His captors took him to their king,
who lived in a big house in the center of the village.

The king apparently ordered him to be destroyed, because the
four warriors led him to the south side of the valley and up a

steep trail to the top of the mountain on the south. Once there he was led to the edge of an overhanging cliff where he could see, some two thousand feet below, huge boulders half-covered by snow and ice. He was permitted only a brief look before two of the warriors grasped his wrists and the other two his ankles and with a "heave ho" launched him into space.

Praying that he might escape a broken bone he made the required count and pulled the rip cord. Fortune was with him, for the north wind carried him away from the boulder-strewn ground and he landed safely in soft new-fallen snow. His luck still held, for less than a mile away he found his collapsed balloon, with everything in the basket untouched, including the food. A day or so later the wind shifted to the south; he moored the balloon to a huge rock, repaired the leak, and reinflated the balloon. He then climbed into the basket and cut the mooring rope. The wind continued from the south and two or three days later he landed safely in Australia.

Such yarns, slightly reminiscent of Jules Verne, were harmless and did much to relieve the boredom of hoeing corn and chopping or picking cotton. Little did we realize that nearly three-quarters of a century later millions of housewives in America would find entertainment by watching on television the unfolding of equally lurid and impossible narratives, while shelling peas for the family dinner or knitting a sweater for an appreciative husband.

6. Play and Playmates

Although my father firmly believed that every child in a family should work for the common good, he was careful not to give us tasks too difficult for our strength. Moreover, he never insisted that we work unreasonably long hours in a day, but I sometimes did not quite agree with his idea of what constituted "unreasonably long hours."

Upon one occasion I was given a grubbing hoe, commonly called a "mattock," and put to work at cutting sprouts in a newly cleared field. That evening at supper, after my father had said grace, I turned my plate over and remarked, "This plate sure feels light after swinging that old mattock all afternoon!"

Father made no reply, but the next morning at breakfast said, "Ed, I think you'd better not cut sprouts today. I'm afraid you'll eat too much dinner and make yourself sick. You can take a hoe and thin corn this morning." Evidently, he thought that he had given me too heavy a job the previous day.

In spite of the fact that George and I started to work at what would today be considered a very early age, we had plenty of time for play. Our father, not being a reading man except for the Bible and his religious paper, had probably never heard of the old adage that "all work and no play makes Jack a dull boy!" but he was wise enough to know that children, like the young of all animals, enjoy playing. He never joined in our games but never objected to them when our work was done.

Sunday was a day of rest, which, to George and me, meant a day of leisure to be devoted largely to playing various games with some of the neighbor boys or merely "horsing around" looking for wild plums and mulberries in the woods or swimming in one of the stock ponds commonly called "tanks." We never attended Sunday School because Father, like most other members of the Old School Baptist Church, objected to the "literature" used in Sunday Schools to explain the various passages of the Scriptures.

The greatest difference between our play and that of present day children was that we had almost no toys except those which we made for ourselves. The greatest treasure of the average Cross Timbers boy of the 1880's was his pocket knife. It was usually a Barlow knife with one blade. George and I each had one, which we whetted to a razor-sharp edge on the sandstone that was abundant on our farm. To lose one's knife was a tragedy. Most little girls had only a doll and sometimes a set of little dishes.

Almost every boy also had a few marbles of various types. The glass ones were called "glassies," plain white ones were either "chalkies" or "connicks," while mottled brown ones were known as "crocks." The superduper or Cadillac of all marbles was an agate. I never owned one, but two or three boys in the neighborhood did and were envied by all the rest of us. The proud possessor of an agate always used it as his "taw." This was a term applied to the marble with which a boy shot at those in the ring or at an opponent's taw after the game was under way. To hit another player's taw removed him from that particular game.

In addition to marbles and a pocket knife, I once received the gift of a small toy pistol and one box of caps. These were about the only "store bought" toys I ever owned. My sister Fannie, in Nebraska, sent us a Christmas box one year containing a bag of beautiful glass marbles for me and a harmonica, which we called a "French harp," for George. He was delighted with this and soon learned to play it very well. The average harmonica cost a quarter and was either a "Hohner" or "Richter" made in Germany.

Although we lacked the toys that children have today, we made many of our own. A good ball could be made from yarn obtained by unraveling an old hand-knitted woolen sock. When the yarn had been rolled up as tightly as possible into a ball, somewhat smaller than a baseball, it had to be thoroughly sewed with a needle and thread or it would unravel. Rubber balls could be bought at a store for from ten to twenty-five cents, but neither George nor I ever felt that we could afford to buy one, even if we had that much money, which was not often.

A sled was easily made upon those rare occasions when there was snow on the ground, and when we could find two or four wheels we often made a small cart or wagon. For use inside the house I would often make a little wagon from four spools and a match box. A wooden pistol could be whittled out of a soft pine board and we often worked at making a bow and some arrows. The bow was usually made either from hickory or Osage orange, called "bode ark" [*bois d'arc*], while straight shafts of false dogwood made excellent arrows. They were scraped down until only slightly thicker than a lead pencil, tipped with a point made of tin, and feathered with bluejay, woodpecker, or mead-ow-lark plumage.

A good bow and half a dozen arrows were highly prized for they represented many hours of patient whittling with a sharp knife and scraping with a piece of broken glass to produce them, and then more time to get the arrows properly tipped and feathered. We hunted with our bows and arrows but I cannot recall that we ever killed anything. Most of our pleasure was derived from shooting at a target and from playing a game with one of us as Robin Hood or William Tell, for our reading af-fected our play just as it did our work. Neither of us ever had enough faith in the other's marksmanship, however, to risk hav-ing an apple shot off his head.

Much of our play with other boys occurred when we had Sun-day visitors, who came to spend the day bringing all the kids with them. A ball was used in several games but my favorite was "town ball," which was a simplified version of baseball. Two self-appointed leaders chose the players for their teams. Who should have first choice was determined by spitting on one side of a small piece of board and calling, "wet or dry?" as it was tossed high in the air. One player called his guess and the two looked at the board when it struck the ground and called, "Dry she lie," or "Wet she lie." If the guess was correct the guesser had first choice, otherwise it went to his opponent. An-other method of deciding who had first choice of players, or which team should bat first, was for one leader to toss either the bat or a stick the size of a broom handle to his opponent. The latter caught it about the middle; the tosser and "tossee" then

clasped the stick hand over hand until the top was reached, and if the lad who reached the top had sufficient grip on the stick to throw it over his shoulder he was the winner. His opponent called, "Venture crow picks!" to prevent its being picked out by thumb and fingers.

In the game itself the ball was pitched rather than thrown and the batter was allowed to have three strikes. He did not have to run, even though he hit the ball the first, or even the second time, that it was pitched to him, if he thought he could do better on his second or third, and final, swing at it. Then he *must* run for first base. If a fielder threw the ball between the runner and the base or "crossed him out," he was out of the game. He was also out if the ball was caught by a player of the other side; any batter who struck at a ball and missed it was out if it was caught by the catcher. Usually when three men were out the opposing team "came to bat." "Town ball" was great fun, especially when there were four or five players on each side and the teams were evenly matched.

Other games played with a ball were "Antony-over," "draw-base," and "work-up," sometimes called "scrub." "Antony-over," sometimes called "anti-over," could be played by any number of players but we seldom had over six or eight at most. They were divided into opposing teams, as in most other games. The two groups lined up on opposite sides of the house or barn. The lad holding the ball called, "Antony" to warn the group on the other side of the building that the ball was coming. They responded by calling, "over" to indicate that they were ready. It should have been easy to catch the ball, but if there were three or four players reaching for it and getting in each others way it often hit the ground. In that case, the same warning was given and the ball was thrown back over the roof.

When a player caught the ball, he streaked around the building, followed by his comrades, and threw the ball at one of the biggest and best players of his opponents as they fled for the opposite side of the barn or house. Any player he hit had to change sides and become a member of his former opponent's team. The game ended when all players had been brought over to one group. We played "Antony-over" using the house as a base only when there was no one inside. Grownups took a very dim view of half a dozen or so kids racing around the outside of the house yelling and laughing, and demanded that we choose some other structure for our game, preferably as far away as possible.

In "draw-base" players were chosen as in most other ball games. Two parallel lines then were drawn on the ground some fifty yards apart. These were "safety lines," behind which the teams stood. A player on one side would throw the ball at the opposing group. If someone caught it he could call any player of the other team over to his own. If the ball was not caught but hit someone the person hit had to run for the line of the opposition. If he reached it safely he became a member of that group. If someone on his own side picked up the ball and hit the runner with it, he had to come back to his own team again.

In "work-up" or "scrub" positions of first batter, second and third batters, pitcher, catcher, right fielder, center and left fielders were assigned by lot. The game was played as in "town ball" but there was usually only one base. If a batter reached it safely he returned to his position, but if put out he started at the bottom as left fielder and every boy in the hierarchy of players then moved up one notch. It was fun and not as complicated as it sounds; but we seldom played it, for there were other games we liked better.

One of these more preferred games was "stink-base," in which two teams were chosen as in "town ball." Two large circles were drawn about seventy-five yards apart. The members of a team were safe as long as they were inside one of these circles. About ten feet from the edge of the part of the circle nearest to the

enemy a line was drawn on the ground called the "dare mark."
If the opposing teams faced north and south, about forty yards
east or west of each circle was a rock or chunk of wood called
"the stink." The chief object of each team was to send one of its
fleetest runners over to touch its opponents' dare mark. When on
such a mission he was immune from attack by the opposition
until the mark was touched.

When he stopped within a foot of the forbidden line he asked,
"Is that your dare mark?"

"Yep," was the answer.

"Doesn't look like much."

"Dare you to touch it though."

The visitor would stick one foot over the dare mark, being
careful not to touch it, and make marks on the ground beyond it
with the heel or toe of his shoe, while the opponents watched
with bated breath, ready to pursue him if he touched the sacred
line. The clever caller would then seek to distract the attention
of his opponents, "Look," he would cry excitedly, as he pointed
his finger toward the house, "you've got company comin'."

If his opponents involuntarily turned their heads, he dragged
his foot across the dare mark and fled for his home base. If caught
he was put on his enemy's "stink," where he had to stay until
rescued by one of his own men running out and touching him
before being touched himself by a runner from the opposition.
If he reached home base safely he and his comrades then had to
guard their own dare mark from being touched by the swiftest
runner of the other team.

The game was varied by one runner calling to his opponents
that he was going around their base. This was often done if his

side had a man or two on "the stink," for in sending out their
fleetest men to capture the runner going around the base, those
who stayed at home might not be able to prevent the rescue of
their prisoners on "the stink."

There were many other outdoor games in which fleetness of
foot was the most desirable quality of every player, including
such simple games as "last-one-on-wood-is-a-bear," and "black
man," sometimes called "wolf-over-the-river." In the latter two
the captains chose their teams as in "town ball," determining
who had first choice by the "wet-or-dry method." Two lines then
were drawn about seventy or eighty yards apart. These were the
safety lines, behind which the opposing teams were lined up. The
captain of one team led his comrades forward as he called,
"What do you do when you see the black man a-comin'?" The
answer was, "Run like a turkey."

The objective of the first black man's team was to catch members of the second group as they spread out and ran to get behind
their opponents' line. When one was caught his captor had to
pat him on the back three times and call out, "One, two, three."
The captive was out of that game and became a member of the
team of his former opponents. The game ended when all of one
side had been caught and what had been two teams had been
merged into one. The winner was of course the original team
that had caught all players of the opposition.

Although we played other "running games" as "sheepy-
sheepy-go" and simple "dare-base" with the "stink" omitted,
probably the most common of all such games was "hide-and-
seek," often called "hide-and-go-seek," "I spy," and even
"whoop-and-hide" by one old lady of our community whose

seven kids were notoriously noisy. Like most other games mentioned, it had slight variations among different families of
children. This was doubtless due to the fact that most of the
people of the Cross Timbers had settled there not many years
before and had come from other states or from different regions
of Texas. Naturally they brought with them customs, idioms,
superstitions, songs, and methods of work and play of the old
homeland as part of their cultural baggage.

Hide-and-seek, as we played it, required the choice of a base,
which might be a large tree or the wall near one corner of a barn.
The original "seeker" might be chosen by drawing straws or by
one of the numerous counting-out rhymes. Our favorite was this
one with the counter pointing his finger at a different player, including himself, with each word.

> Monkey, monkey, bottle o' beer
> How many monkeys have we here.
> One, two, three
> Out goes *he*.

The one designated as *he* stepped aside and the rhyme was re-
peated until all players were out but one, who became "it."

He put his face against the tree or wall at the corner of the
barn designated, closed his eyes, and began to count slowly. At
100 he called loudly, "A bushel o' wheat and a bushel o' rye, all
that ain't hid holler I."

Usually everyone had found a hiding place behind a corn crib
or a clump of bushes, or by lying flat on the ground behind a rail
fence or cellar. If some slowpoke was not yet hidden he yelled
"I." The counter then continued to 120 and then called again,

"A bushel o' wheat and a bushel o' clover, all that ain't hid can't hide over. All eyes open!"

He then set out in search of the hidden players. When one was found a race for the base followed. If the counter reached it first he slapped it three times with his hand and called, "One, two, three for John." If the hidden one got there first it was *he* that patted the base three times as he called, "One, two, three for *me*." This rule of slapping the base three times no doubt was to avoid disputes as to which one won the race if it happened to be very close.

The counter continued his search until all players had won the race or had been caught. The game was then resumed with the first player caught as "it." The game was great fun and children of all ages, including both boys and girls, played it. There were minor variations, as in most other games. Some families of kids who called the game "I spy" called, "I spy Billy, one, two, three," but it was still fundamentally "hide-and-seek."

Many other games were played, including "corn-cob-battle," in which sides were chosen and every player was armed with corn cobs. Any player struck with a cob was "dead" and out of the battle. Another game, no doubt of English origin, was called "How-many-miles-to-Miley Bright?" In this a safety line was drawn some two hundred yards from the starting point. All players, but two or three, started for the line but soon met a traveler and asked, "How many miles to Miley Bright?"

"Three score and ten."

"Can we get there by candlelight?"

"If your legs are long and your heels are light."

As the group moved on, the lone traveler called a warning, "Look out for witches on the way!"

A little farther on, one or two "witches" hidden in the bushes beside the road suddenly dashed out and tried to catch the fleeing pilgrims before they reached the safety line. The game was then resumed with the first two caught playing the part of witches.

Other games were "what's-your-trade," no doubt the ancestor of "What's My Line?," and less strenuous ones, such as pitching horseshoes, or tossing marbles at a line. The latter, called "lagging-marbles," was often played for "keeps," meaning that the pitcher whose marble was closer to the line kept both of them. I seldom played marbles for keeps, partly because it seemed to be gambling, and also because one could go broke very quickly.

Although we always liked to play outside with other boys, George and I were often forced to play alone and in bad weather we had to stay inside. Yet, I cannot recall that we were ever bored. On rainy days we might play checkers on a board made by ourselves on the wooden lid of a candy bucket, using lima beans and buttons or grains of corn for checker men. We also popped corn and roasted peanuts and sometimes played "ranching." We had two or three rag rugs on the floor and one of these became the ranch. Big white grains of popcorn were sheep, peanuts or pecans were cattle, and marbles were horses. We bought and sold livestock, traded cattle for sheep or vice versa, and swapped a horse for more cows, pausing sometimes to "kill a beef" or a couple of sheep.

We played "hull gull" with pecans, peanuts, or grains of popcorn, setting a limit of ten as the number that could be used in each play. For example, if peanuts were to be used the first player could take any number of not more than ten concealed in his cupped hands, shake them in front of his opponent, and say, "hull gull"; the response was "hand full."

"How many?" asked the first player. If the guess made by the second player was correct he won the peanuts. If it was wrong he must give the first player as many peanuts as the difference between his guess and the correct number.

One day George and I found an ad in the *Farm and Fireside* of "One game dominoes, one game authors, six hidden-name cards, all for ten cents." It seemed such a bargain that we pooled our financial resources and mailed our dime to the company. In a week or so the package came. The games consisted of two large sheets of paper; one was black on one side with the dominoes printed on it in white ink. A leaflet instructed us to paste the sheet on thick cardboard and cut out the dominoes with scissors or a sharp knife. The other sheet was white with the names of authors enclosed in small squares. They had no "stickem" on them, but we mixed a paste of flour and water and carefully pasted the domino sheet to a large piece of cardboard. Once it was fixed firmly to the cardboard base and was fully dry came the ticklish job of cutting out the dominoes. When that was completed we had a good set of dominoes, which we used for a year or more. The game of authors we felt was not worth the trouble.

Our playmates changed from time to time as farms were sold or renters moved away and new farmers took their places. The Clarks, like the poor, we "had with us always" but, while they sometimes played "town ball" or some other game with us, they were far from being our favorite comrades.

Almost from the time we moved to the Cross Timbers farm the Brileys, already mentioned, were among our closest friends. When they came to see us on Sunday and spent the day we had a great deal of fun playing marbles or ball with their boys, Walter and Oscar. Sometimes we did not play games but roamed about the farm seeking wild berries. George was a year or so older than Walter and frequently played tricks on him and Oscar, in which I might be either an accessory or a fellow victim.

On one occasion the four of us were in the orchard eating peaches when we were joined by Bill and Ben Clark. In the near-by garden grew a couple of rows of winter onions called "shal-lots." George and I had discovered that by pinching off the tip of one of these onion blades and bruising an inch of that end we could make noises faintly resembling music by blowing through the hollow tube and striking the wilted end with a finger.

I was diligently playing one of these "onion trumpets" when George suggested that he and the other boys put on an Indian dance. They joined hands and danced about in a circle emitting a few "yippees" to accompany my so-called music. When George proposed that they all close their eyes and dance, they readily agreed. They had not noticed a big bull nettle growing nearby until both Oscar and Ben Clark at the same instant gave two wild war whoops as they broke away from the circle of dancers and began to rub their bare feet and shins!

Oscar Briley squalled easily, which only caused us to play more pranks on him than on other boys. We were playing "town ball"

one morning and I still recall the momentary shocked look on his
mother's face when I rushed into the house, apparently much
excited, and exclaimed, "Mrs. Briley, Oscar got hit in the back
of the head with the ball and the bawl came out of his mouth!"

On another Sunday when the Brileys were visiting us Oscar
went in the house to look through a new book of pictures. While
he was gone George and Walter got a spade and we hastily dug
a hole about three feet long, a foot and a half wide, and a foot
deep; we filled this with water and put some dry brittle sticks
across it. We then laid dry leaves across these and carefully
covered them with dirt. After sweeping the surplus earth away
we had a neat, slightly raised plane three feet long and about
eighteen inches wide.

The work was barely finished when Oscar, having looked at
all the pictures, came out to find us engaged in a jumping con-
test. We had drawn a line on the ground about as far from our
booby trap as we thought Oscar could jump. As he came up
George, Walter, and I in turn all jumped but all fell a little short
of the goal.

"I can beat that a lot," bragged Oscar and proved it by squar-
ing away and jumping entirely over the trap which we had so
carefully laid. Evidently all was lost unless Oscar could be persuaded to jump from a line farther back, which might arouse his
suspicions. George was equal to the emergency. "That's fine,
Oscar," he said blandly, "but the one who jumps exactly *on* that
raised place on the ground does a *little* better than if he jumps
clear over it." Because Oscar wanted to do as well as he could
he jumped again and landed in the middle of the raised ground
with disastrous results.

My brother George's crowning act of infamy came later when we were out at the cow lot and discovered a bird's nest high up in a fairly tall tree. Walter was urged to climb up to see if there were eggs or young birds in it. The climb was not an easy one, because the tree had no branches for the first ten or twelve feet and the trunk was unusually smooth. Walter gripped it with his legs and arms, however, and with a boost from George eventually reached the first limb and from there on he had no difficulty.

Walter reached the nest and called down to us that it was empty. As he started to climb down George seized a one-by-four piece of lumber about ten feet long that was leaning against the fence, dipped the end of it in a large soft "cow puddin'," and smeared the tree trunk liberally as far up as he could reach. Walter yelled frantically, "Oh, *Girge, Girge,*" as he saw his descent to earth so effectually blocked.

The rest of us laughed heartily, but when he started crying we began to realize that the incident might have serious consequences for George. Oscar and I were innocent bystanders but we might be deemed guilty by association, and our plea that we had no idea of George's intentions when he "got Walter up a tree" as he did, might fall on deaf ears. Personally I doubted that George's act was premeditated. It seems more likely that he yielded to temptation when he saw Walter high in the tree and the means of keeping him there so close at hand.

Getting Walter down proved to be a difficult task. We piled a mound of hay beneath the tree and urged him to jump on top of it, but it looked like too long a drop and he refused. Finally, George climbed up partway and helped Walter down, both of them getting more or less messed up before Walter was safe on the ground again. They cleaned up as best they could and I heard George say, "We won't let the folks know what a mess we got ourselves into, will we, Walter?" To this Walter replied, "Oh, no! Of course we won't!" I am sure that neither of them ever did.

We were truly sorry when the Brileys moved to Roanoke and a year later migrated to the Prairie West. We never saw any of the family again but rumors reached us that they were doing well as wheat growers in western Oklahoma or the Texas Panhandle.

We had numerous other playmates but none who could quite take the place of Walter and Oscar. One of them was Bob Kemp, a brother of Mrs. Jake West, whose husband had bought the old Blodgett farm. We did not play with Bob much because he had lived in Fort Worth and was more or less a town kid. Bill Mayes, whose parents lived on the prairie a short distance west of us; Sumter Boone, whose Dad lived at what was called "Boone P'int"; and the Bourland brothers, Andy, Ed, and Sam, were among our good boy friends.

By far our closest friends during the latter years of our life in the Cross Timbers were the twin brothers, Paul and Dow Taylor, mentioned in an earlier chapter. They were lads after our own hearts, for they did not chew tobacco or smoke cigarettes as did many boys of the community. Moreover, they liked to read, never swore or used bad language, were always courteous, and yet were by no means sissies; we were therefore always glad to be with them.

Yet, much as we liked the company of other boys and playing games with them, we were always able to entertain ourselves when alone. Perhaps the fact that we had plenty of work to do in the fields and around the house made any leisure hours sweeter and helped keep us from ever being bored. Even though we had no toys except a jack knife, a few marbles, and a homemade ball, it would never have occurred to us to ask our elders, "What can I do?" Our only problem was which of the many activities open to us promised the most fun.

Many games can be played by only two and we knew them all, including marbles, "hide-and-seek," pitching horseshoes, and mumble-peg, in which the loser must pull a peg from the ground with his teeth. The loser, however, had the privilege of responding to the driver's question, "Three with 'em open or five with 'em shut?" This referred to number of blows with the knife on the peg and whether the driver made them with his eyes open or closed.

There were two forms of mumble-peg, but the penalty suffered by the loser was the same in each. In the first type points ranging from five to a hundred were given for the position in which the knife was made to fall; the first player to secure five hundred points won the game.

In the second and more complicated game the winner was the first to complete a long series of throws. Each player sought to leave the single blade of the knife sticking in the ground with the handle upright. When a player failed in a throw his opponent took over and continued until he too failed. The plays of holding the blade between the thumb and each finger of the right hand in turn and of holding the knife point against fist, elbow, shoulder, nose, and chin were fairly easy.

They became increasingly difficult, however, when the player must throw the knife from various positions. These had specific names, such as "break the chicken's neck," "shave old Pete,"

"mark the pigs," "help the lady over the fence," and "knock sky
winders," sometimes called "spank the baby's rear" because the
handle of the knife was placed on the player's knee and the flat
side of the blade projecting into space was struck sharply with
the edge of the hand. The final throw, called "find the goose's
nest," was made by the player holding the blade in his hand and
throwing the knife straight back over his head.

We frequently played games suggested by our reading, each
of us shifting his role to another character when necessary. On
one occasion we were playing King Solomon's Mines, in which
we crossed a newly plowed field, which was the desert, and
climbed the corn crib, which was the mountain designated in
the book as "Sheba's left breast." We stopped before reaching
the top when we found in the cave the frozen body of the Por-
tuguese, who had died so many years before.

After some discussion of our find we continued our journey,
passed over the summit of the mountain, and descended to the
valley beyond it. Here I dropped the role of Sir Henry Curtis and
assumed that of the chief of the hostile natives. Running on
ahead I pulled up a stalk of sorghum cane from a nearby stack of
feed and with a whoop of defiance threw my spear at these in-
truders. Unfortunately, our father, who had been visiting one of
the neighbors, came around the corner of "Sheba's breast" just
then and attracted George's attention. As a result, my well-aimed
spear hit his cheek, breaking the skin and making a long red
mark.

This rang down the curtain on King Solomon's Mines instantly. I stammered that we were only playing a game, but Father
did not seem to appreciate any such games. He knew that it was

an accident but suggested that I either go inside and study my spelling book or play some less dangerous game. I was deeply penitent, knowing that if my spear had struck George's eye the result might have been very serious.

Although I missed George more than I can find words to express when we were separated even for a few days, and I think he missed me; yet, it was possible for me to play alone in quite happy fashion. It seems certain that reading stimulated our imaginations, and the fact that we worked fairly hard made us appreciate leisure. In addition, we had virtually no toys except those which we made for ourselves. Perhaps these were the chief factors in keeping us contented, happy, and never at a loss for something to do.

7. Young Nimrods

When George was about twelve years old he began to develop a great yearning for a gun. There was not very much game in our part of the Cross Timbers, but the desire to own a gun and go hunting seems to be born in every farm boy and may have been stronger in the 1880's than it is today.

In the large attic bedroom where George and I slept was an old musket of the Civil War vintage. Unfortunately, the tube on which the percussion cap rests had been broken off, probably on my father's journey from Missouri to Nebraska or from that state to Texas. We never asked Father to give us the history of that ancient firearm. It may have been given to him when he was a member of the Northern Home Guard or possibly he had bought it after the War from a dealer in surplus army material.

George was not interested in the pedigree of the old shooting iron. His only concern was in getting it fixed so that it would be usable again. The nearest gunsmith was in Fort Worth, but a blacksmith at Roanoke claimed that he had formerly worked on guns a little. He added that he had a catalogue from a company in St. Louis that sold guns and supplied parts for almost every type of firearm.

Once he had learned this, our father yielded to George's earnest pleas and delivered "the old musket," as we always called it, to this worthy blacksmith to be fitted with a new tube. A couple of weeks later it was ready and Father, who had gone to Roanoke with a few bushels of sweet potatoes, brought it home.

George was delighted. Not only did it have a new tube but all traces of rust had been removed and the stock and metal parts polished until they shone. His joy was brief. When he pulled the hammer back something snapped in the lock and the hammer became limp. A hasty examination showed that the mainspring had broken.

This was truly a tragedy but the friendly blacksmith was equal to the emergency. Somewhere he found another lock, which by a little careful trimming of the wooden space into which it must be fitted was entirely satisfactory. Once more Father brought the old gun home and once more George made joyful noises and began to assemble equipment for hunting.

Our friends Paul and Dow Taylor had presented us with two beautiful powder horns. One was used for powder and the other for shot. An empty brass shell of a rifle cartridge could be used as a "charger" to measure the quantity of powder and shot to be used in loading the old gun. Since the percussion caps for a musket were large and had a rim around the bottom we called them "hat caps." They came in a round tin box containing a hundred.

Father had brought a box of caps, a half pound of powder, and a pound of shot when he returned from Roanoke with the old musket. The next day was Saturday and he was going to the Denton Creek Church, which had preaching both Saturday and Sunday. The members were so few and so widely scattered that services were held only once a month, with two days devoted to preaching.

It was early October and we had just about finished the first picking of cotton. Knowing our eagerness to try out the old musket, Father told us that we could quit at noon the next day and go hunting. He warned us to be careful in handling the gun and told us that while hunting in the woods one should stop from time to time to look and listen. He added that the Indian knew that if he waited patiently the game would come to him.

We were up early as usual the next morning and as soon as breakfast was over George and I headed for the cotton field, leaving Father to saddle old Pompey and start for the Denton Creek Church. It was a beautiful day but the morning seemed long. We told stories to entertain ourselves a little, but we had no heart for either telling or listening. It was fortunate that both of us did not get cricks in our necks from looking up at the sun so often to estimate how long it would be until noon. During our ten years of life in the Cross Timbers, I cannot recall that we ever had what was locally called a "timepiece." In fair weather we judged time by the sun, and at night or in cloudy weather by guess.

At long last when George had decided that it must be about noon we emptied our cotton sacks and hurried to the house. By the time we had washed, Alice had dinner ready. We swallowed our food hastily, and then gathered up the powder horns, box of caps, brass charger, a bunch of paper for wadding, and a game bag of all-too-generous proportions, which Alice had made for us. Certain that we had everything we needed, George shouldered the old gun, and we set out on our first hunt with as much enthusiasm as two African explorers starting on their first safari.

Perhaps it is not correct to say "we" started. George was the hunter and I, only seven years old, could claim no higher rank than that of the "number-one boy," trailing along some three paces behind and to the right. George carried the gun, about the same length as himself, over his right shoulder except in the woods where game was momentarily expected to be seen. Then it was held with the stock under his right arm, finger on the trigger, thumb on the hammer, and the central part of the stock held in the left hand. This was "at ready," for the muzzle was pointed ahead and downward at an angle of about forty-five degrees.

The powder and shot horns hung at his left side, the box of caps and metal charger rattled slightly in one pants pocket, and a hip pocket bulged with a bunch of newspapers. My only duties were to carry the game bag and game, if any; to walk softly; to keep quiet; and to look and listen for quails, squirrels, rabbits, or any other game.

We crossed the orchard and entered the woods to the north of it. Quite a large stretch of woodland here extended north to a road running east and west between the Clark and Taylor farms. In the woods were many dense thickets of underbrush interlaced with greenbrier and sarsaparilla vines. These furnished excellent homes for rabbits and coveys of quail, being almost impenetrable for hawks and nearly as difficult for human enemies with guns to infiltrate. Here we jumped three or four rabbits, but they scurried away so fast that there was no chance for a shot at one.

Doubling back to the edge of our own east field we saw a few doves; when one alighted on a nearby tree George raised the old musket and fired. Down came the bird and we had our first item for the capacious game bag. George was very proud of his marksmanship but I later came to realize that he could hardly

have missed, as the dove was scarcely twenty-five yards away.

We continued our hunt, turning north through a long stretch of fairly open timber. This was not good quail territory, but we again jumped several cottontail rabbits. All of them scampered away, however, and my brother had no intentions of wasting powder and shot on any moving target. His attitude was like that of Dow Taylor, who later remarked to me, "You know Ed, lots of times I can't hit 'em when they're sittin' still."

At long last, a young cottontail hopped out of a small thicket and paused to look around before deciding which way to run. It was a fatal mistake. The old musket spoke again and George dashed forward to pick up the kicking rabbit, bang its head against a tree, and hand it to me for the game bag. As by this time it was growing late we started for home because in Father's absence we had to do all the evening chores, including milking two cows. When we entered the thick woods north of the orchard George suddenly stopped. I could hear a slight rustling of the dry leaves in a thicket some twenty yards ahead of us but could see nothing. Evidently George, who was three or four steps ahead of me could, however, for he fired and a dozen or more quails flew up from the thicket. George dropped the gun and ran at full speed to retrieve his game.

"How many did you get George?" I called as he dropped to his knees and reached out with both hands to seize the still fluttering quails.

"One, two, three of 'em," he exclaimed excitedly as he got to his feet and brought the birds back to me to be put in the game bag.

"You sure did run fast to pick 'em up after you shot!"

"That's the way to do," he replied. "If you don't get there quick, a crippled one may run off. When you shoot any game you've got to run to pick it up. Sometimes you'll just stun a rabbit or squirrel and he'll get up and run off if you don't run and pick him up right *now!*"

This ended our first day's hunt, and we hurried home to show the results to Alice, who was quite impressed by our success. In fact, we were quite proud of our afternoon's work ourselves.

George's haste to retrieve his game reminded me of a yarn told by our brother Tom. He said that a certain man who was very good at throwing rocks complained that he could knock a rabbit over with a rock at twenty or thirty yards very easily, but it always got up and ran away before he could get to it. A friend told him to run faster and seize the rabbit before it recovered from the shock. He was then more successful, but eventually he developed so much speed that one day he threw at a rabbit and ran so fast to pick it up that the rock came along and hit him in the back!!

We found later that bagging three quails, one dove, and one rabbit on our first afternoon of hunting was a case of "beginner's luck." For the next few months we hunted most of our spare time, but if the household had been forced to rely upon the game we brought in for its meat supply the entire family would have become largely vegetarians. Yet, we never grew discouraged. Any day when it was too wet to pick cotton and we were not busy with other work, we were in the woods and fields with George carrying the gun while I tagged along behind.

Moreover, to us "meat was meat," as the old-time plainsmen used to say. There were no game laws, no closed season, and no bag limits, although the last named would not have affected us. George shot quails, squirrels, rabbits, doves, meadow larks, and once a prairie chicken, of which he was very proud.

For some three months I was fairly content to accept the role of game-bag bearer and general assistant for George. If we sighted a squirrel in a tree, however, I could be a real help by going to the opposite side of the tree and making enough noise to induce the squirrel to slip around to the side of the trunk where George stood with the gun ready for a shot. This tendency of a squirrel to keep the tree trunk between himself and the hunter created endless debate as to whether a man going around the tree went around the squirrel!

It was always fun to go hunting with George doing all the shooting, but eventually I developed a yen to test my own marksmanship with the old musket. February 8 was my eighth birthday. Early in the afternoon Alice went over to see Mrs. Clark, George had been sent to Keller on an errand, and Father was grubbing out stumps in the far side of a newly cleared field. It looked to me like a golden opportunity to celebrate my birthday by going hunting.

Very carefully I took the old musket from the rack on the wall, which George had made to hold it. I then stuffed paper in one pocket, the box of caps and charger in another, and with powder and shot horns hanging from a strap over my left shoulder and the old gun over the right one. I sallied forth in search of game.

The old musket was loaded and so was I—with all the impediments to carry, plus a gun considerably longer than myself. I crossed one corner of the field east of the orchard and entered the dense woods where George had killed the three quails on our first-day's hunt. My fondest hope was to find another covey of quail and mow down at least four or five at one shot.

If I had met with such good fortune it is doubtful if anyone could have lived with me for the next month or so with any degree of comfort. Fortunately, for my family and playmates, Lady Luck was not with me nor were the shades of Diana, Nimrod, Daniel Boone, Buffalo Bill, or any other great hunters of the past. Neither quails, rabbits, nor squirrels came in view. At last a bright-colored bird which we called a "yellowhammer," doubtless a flicker, alighted on the branch of a tree not over fifty or sixty feet away. In desperation I eased my conscience by saying to myself that the plumage would be excellent to feather my arrows. The gun was too heavy for me to hold up but I rested it in the fork of a bush, sighted along the barrel, and pulled the trigger.

At the report of the gun the bird fell dead, for it would have been almost impossible to miss at that range. I reloaded the gun very carefully but decided to call it a day and go home. My father said that he saw me heading for the woods with the gun and was a little uneasy but decided not to stop me. Neither George nor Alice seemed to think it unusual for a boy of my age to go hunting with an old musket, but today most mothers and fathers would faint at the sight of their eight-year-old son-and-heir headed for the woods with a man-size gun.

Within a few months we found that the spring in the lock of the old musket was hardly strong enough to explode the big "hat caps," but frequently snapped. Moreover, the big musket caps were not carried in stock by our local stores, as the double-

barrel muzzle-loading shotgun was the favorite type of gun in
the Cross Timbers. George and I, therefore, spent many hours
patiently filing down the tube of our old gun until it was small
enough to accommodate the standard-size percussion caps made
for shotguns.

When spring came a great many migratory plovers stopped
over on the prairies for a short time before continuing their flight
north. Also, there was a large increase in the number of doves
and larks, although some of both these birds, especially larks,
remained on the prairie adjoining our section of the Cross Timbers all winter.

The old musket was our only gun until Alice and I took the
train for the West in October, 1888. When Father and George
joined us some six weeks later they brought with them a double-
barrel muzzle-loading shotgun. George explained to me that
they had traded a cow for it and that the old musket had again
been relegated to the attic bedroom.

George stayed in Greer County only three or four months and
went hunting with Henry only two or three times. The only time
that I went with them was on a hunt for turkeys on the nearby
Indian Reservation. Here were huge flocks of turkeys, which increased very rapidly because of the Indians' taboo against eating
them.

We took a wagon and team, crossed the river which was the
Reservation boundary, and camped on the eastern branch of Otter
Creek, which was called Dry Otter because it seldom had any
water in it except immediately after a heavy rain. It was near
sunset when we stopped to camp, and looking up stream we were
thrilled to see a long file of wild turkeys moving along in the

edge of the timber, which bordered the creek. They were not over two or three hundred yards away and clearly would be going to roost in the trees within an hour at most. Henry, who had been a professional hunter, said that we should make camp and cook supper. By the time we had eaten, it would be dark and the turkeys roosting in the trees could be easily shot.

Unfortunately, soon after dark we heard from up the creek the noise of a great flapping of turkey wings. Henry declared that the big birds had gone to roost but had been distrurbed by some prowling animal, probably either a bobcat or a panther. We waited an hour for them to get settled down again. Then, hoping that they had not traveled too far, we started up the dry, sandy bed of the creek in search of them.

Henry and George were in front with the guns, and I trudged along behind. It was hard walking on the loose sand, and although we walked for what seemed to me several miles the great flock of turkeys had completely disappeared. Henry took one shot at a dark object near the top of a tree, but it proved to be only the empty nest of a squirrel! At long last we despaired of finding the huge flock of turkeys and made our way back to camp. When we finally reached it I could barely put one foot in front of the other. The next morning we returned to Navajoe, as Henry had to get back to work.

Obviously this expedition had nothing to do with hunting in the Cross Timbers, but it gave me an experience to relate with considerable embellishments to my young associates when we returned to our own home a few months later.

Soon after this brief hunting trip George returned to the Cross Timbers to work for our brother Tom. He did not take the shotgun with him, as he rode down to Vernon, Texas, with Henry and from there by train to Keller. When Father and I followed him by wagon a few months later the old double-barrel gun proved most useful. It was early June and the spring crop of young rabbits, about half-grown, was good. During the entire journey of ten days we had fried young rabbit for supper almost every evening and found it equal to fried chicken.

For a few weeks after reaching our destination we were too busy helping Tom to get any hunting done, but during the weeks we stayed at the Briley house we had little to do except feed and water the pigs and milk the cows. Although it was hot as the hinges of Hereafter, we spent most of the time ranging the woods in search of game. Here we were farther down in the woods and there were some groves of hickory trees, so that the red squirrels were quite numerous.

Later, when we went out to Parker County and camped on Walnut Creek, George and I spent every day that was too damp to pick cotton hunting along the stream. A good many coveys of quail were in the thickets near the banks of the creek or in the edges of the nearby fields. In addition, we found more squirrels here than in our home community, for there were more walnut trees to supply them with winter food.

While we were picking the overflowed field of cotton for Mr. Chandler, Father went up to his house one day on some errand. When he returned to camp he reported with some interest that Chandler had a genuine old Kentucky squirrel rifle and had suggested that he might be willing to trade it for our double-barrel shotgun.

"I haven't seen one like it for years," Father said with considerable enthusiasm. "It's just the kind of gun I always wanted when I was younger. Of course if you boys want to keep the shotgun we won't trade, but I wanted to tell you about it."

Both George and I were intrigued by the idea of getting a different gun. The locks of the old shotgun were getting a bit weak so that it sometimes snapped, usually at the most critical time. We assured Father that a trade would be all right with us.

The next day Mr. Chandler brought the rifle down to camp and as we examined it our enthusiasm grew. It was considerably longer than the old musket and had a "full stock," that is, reaching nearly to the end of the long octagonal barrel. It also had set triggers, and the mountings on the shoulder plate and elsewhere were of polished brass. It looked brand new, although it must have been made soon after percussion caps came in to replace the earlier flintlock guns. The exact caliber we never knew, but a bullet mold that came with it indicated that it was about .25.

Mr. Chandler suggested at first that he should have about $2.50 "to boot," in Cross Timbers lingo. Father in reply questioned whether either gun was worth that much; at last Chandler agreed to an even trade. George was much pleased with the exchange and was very proud of his new gun, which at least attracted the attention and interest of everyone who saw it.

Soon after this transaction had been completed we packed our possessions in the wagon and returned to Tom and Lucy's place. A few weeks later, when we gained possession of our own home, almost my first act was to resurrect the old musket from the attic bedroom. I set to work polishing it up, as it apparently had not been touched since we left home.

From that time until we left the Cross Timbers home nearly

three years later the old musket was my gun, while the long squirrel rifle was George's personal property. We bought bars of lead to be melted and moulded into bullets. Because these were carried in a small leather pouch George gave me the horn in which we had been accustomed to carrying shot. I used this for powder and made myself a new horn for shot, using a small saw to cut off the ends smoothly, patiently scraping with pieces of glass, and whittling with my knife.

With a gun each, George and I continued to hunt together when neither of us had to be at work. George with his long rifle specialized on squirrels, jack rabbits, and cotton tails, while I with the old scattergun watched with eager eyes for coveys of quail or doves, plovers, and larks. Eventually I became fairly good at handling the old musket and would sometimes knock down a running rabbit.

If George happened to be busy I often hunted alone; even from the first, neither my father nor anyone else ever questioned my ability to hunt alone with complete safety to myself, some other person, or livestock. I was ten years old, "going on eleven," and was considered old enough to take care of myself.

Sometimes if I came near a road passers-by seeing my small figure lugging the long gun seemed surprised and started joshing me a bit. Usually they would yell something like this: "Hey kid! Ain't that gun too big for ye?" "Whadda you expect to kill? You don't need to load a gun that long, time you get in range you kin just punch 'em to death!" I paid no attention to such good-natured razzing for "words could not hurt me."

I wish it were possible for me to say truthfully that we met with some surprising adventure in our hunting but we did not.

While I recall seeing one wolf, he was far away and getting farther every second. The game which we bagged consisted only of rabbits, squirrels, quails, plovers, doves, larks, an occasional prairie chicken or duck, and sometimes an opposum. A few foxes and raccoons were in these woods but we never saw one, for they slept in a den or hollow tree by day and came out to seek food only at night.

Yet, hunting was fun and had for George and me many "fringe benefits." Not only was it good, healthful exercise to tramp the woods, fields, and prairies carrying a heavy gun but it taught me, at least, at a very early age how to handle a gun with safety to myself and others. Constant watching for game sharpened our eyes and ears and made us close observers of the plant life. We came to know the common names of all the trees, shrubs, vines, flowers, and types of grass in that part of the Cross Timbers.

Moreover, we learned much of the habits and lifeways not only of the game we sought, but of all wild creatures of the woodlands. Perhaps we did not "learn of every bird its language," as did little Hiawatha, but we did learn to recognize the songs and cries of virtually all birds of this part of the Cross Timbers. We also came to learn the type of nest that each built and the number and color of the eggs.

Finally, I think that hunting taught us to love and respect the wild creatures of the forest and to have humanity toward them. We hunted for food. All birds or animals that could not be eaten were perfectly safe from our guns. In addition, we always did our best to stop any boy who wanted to bang away at any bird in sight, even a cardinal, bluebird, sparrow, blue jay, mockingbird, scissor tail, woodpecker, or anything else. Such birds we always did our best to protect.

We tried to be sure of our game before shooting, and if we wounded a bird we would spend hours searching for it, instead of going on to let it die by inches. Upon one occasion I found a mud hen with an injured wing. I took it home, bound up its broken wing, put it in a coop, and fed and watered it twice a day. In a week or ten days the injured wing was healed, and when the hen was able to fly we took it to a large stock pond and released it.

We never hunted on Sunday, but Saturday afternoon often found us in the woods with the old musket and long rifle, especially in the winter. On the whole, I have always felt that my hours devoted to hunting were well spent and taught me much that was very useful in my later life.

8. Disciples of St. Peter and Izaak Walton

My father never seemed to take much interest in hunting but sometimes boasted a little on his ability as a fisherman. He seldom went fishing with us but upon those rare occasions when he did he usually made good on his claims to being something of an expert in the art of angling. At least he usually caught more fish than any of the rest of us.

Fishing for George and me was confined to the streams within walking distance of home. This meant only three: Marshall Branch, the upper part of which was hardly a mile to the north; Henrietta Creek, a much larger stream about three miles to the west of our home; and Bear Creek, which had its source near Keller and flowed eastward, presumably into the Trinity River.

Marshall Branch and Henrietta Creek ran north into a much larger stream called Denton Creek. We were told that it and the county and town of Denton were named for himself by an early pioneer settler of that area. It was also said that he had three daughters, Henrietta, Elizabeth, and the baby girl, little Harriet, and that he named the three southern tributaries of Denton Creek for them. If so, he erred in naming the westernmost of the three tributaries "Little Harriet Creek," for it is the biggest of the three!

While George and I hunted in summer as well as winter, as there were no closed seasons, we usually preferred fishing during the spring and summer months, though we sometimes took the gun or guns with us even when going fishing. Always there was the possibility that we might see some ducks, plovers, rabbits, or some other game.

Marshall Branch, being the nearest fishing stream, was visited far more often than Henrietta Creek; I do not recall ever fishing in Bear Creek, but George did at least a few times with some boys of his own age. We seldom fished more than four or five times a summer in Henrietta Creek and always spent the entire day, taking a lunch with us.

Our fishing tackle was very simple. All we ever had was a long willow pole with a line, hook, sinker of lead, and a large cork, usually from a pickle bottle, for a "bobber." We punched a hole in the middle of the cork, through which the line ran, and then moved the cork up or down depending upon the depth of the water. We had seen reels but never dreamed of using one; and flies, plugs, spinners, spoons, snell hooks, leaders, minnow buckets, landing nets, creels, casting rods, fly rods, and all the other gadgets that fishermen use now, we had never seen.

If we needed a stringer we made one by tying one end of a yard-length of line around the middle of a green stick the size of a lead pencil. The other end of the line we tied close to one end of a short green stick that was sharpened to a point at its other end so that it could be easily passed through the gills and out of the mouth of any fish caught. The sharpened stick could then be pushed into the ground near the edge of the water to serve as an anchor to all fish we had landed.

For bait we used earthworms, sometimes called redworms or fishworms. Lacking these we used grasshoppers, crickets, grub-worms, liver, or the flesh of a bird or rabbit which we had shot. Some persons asserted that small balls of dough or a bit of red flannel might be used as bait for catching certain kinds of fish.

Many superstitions were applied to fishing and wide differ-ences of opinion were held as to how and when one could have the best luck in fishing. Fletcher Williams and other boys in the neighborhood would always spit on the bait before putting the hook in the water. Other fishermen thought that the direction from which the wind was blowing influenced one's luck in fish-ing, and these quoted a little rhyme:

> Wind's in the east,
> The fish bite the least.
> Wind from the south,
> Blows the hook from their mouth.
> Wind in the west,
> The fish bite the best.

Still others declared that the moon had something to do with one's luck in fishing but apparently they could never agree on whether it was better in the light or dark of the moon. Con-siderable difference of opinion also prevailed as to the time of day when the fish were most likely to be biting, though it was generally conceded that early morning and late afternoon were better than the middle of the day.

My brother George and I had little faith in such ideas but fished any time during the spring and summer months that we were free from work, which was usually Saturday afternoon. As

Marshall Branch was within easy walking distance it was our favorite fishing stream when we had only a half day to fish. It traversed a short-grass prairie region with two or three trees and a few clumps of willows on its banks for a mile or two from its source near the railroad.

We usually dug a can of worms and started fishing on the upper reaches of the stream and fished down it for a couple of miles, since the so-called "fishing holes" became progressively larger and deeper as we got farther downstream. The water was usually a little cloudy, at least compared with the much larger Henrietta Creek.

We had no particular rules to follow in fishing except to set the float or "bobber" on the line high enough to let the hook come within a few inches of the bottom of the pool. If set so high that the hook lay on the bottom crawfish would steal the bait. We never spat on the bait, for that we regarded as a foolish superstition, but we were careful to bait the hook in such a way as to keep the point covered.

Once the baited hook was in the water it was necessary only to watch the cork, and when it went under or started moving across the water to jerk quickly and pull out the fish. Of course you sometimes lost one which you always felt was bigger than the largest one you caught. At least that was what you told your comrade and the folks at home!

We caught plenty of fish in Marshall Branch but they were small. Most of them were perch, bream, sunfish, and catfish so small that we often referred to them as "kitten fish." Once in a while we might catch one a foot long but the average length was

about seven to nine inches. We often caught as many as forty
or more fish in a single afternoon but three-fourths of them
would be perch, bream, and sunfish. Rolled in corn meal and
fried in deep fat, however, they were quite good eating.

Fishing in Henrietta Creek was more fun, and more of an adventure than in Marshall Branch. It was not only a much larger
stream but it was in a limestone area and the water was usually
very clear. Also, because it was bordered by large trees it was
possible to sit on a rock in the shade and watch comfortably, as
well as patiently, your cork floating on the water.

The first fishing trip to Henrietta Creek that I can recall was
when by brother Henry visited us before he had joined Mattie's
husband in establishing a store at Navajoe. In addition to bringing us a caged prairie dog, a pair of kangaroo rats, and a lot of
dried turkey meat, he had in his wagon a "trammel net." When
he proposed that we go fishing our father, George, and I accompanied him to Henrietta Creek.

A trammel net consists of two nets, one with large holes and
the other with small holes. After it is stretched across a stream
the fishermen go upstream some thirty yards and drive the fish
toward the net by wading downstream. The fish go through the
large holes and strike the smaller meshed net, which stops them.

The two nets are so close together that the fish cannot turn
completely around and are caught between the two when the net
is pulled out of the water. We made a good catch that day,
hauling up three or four drum, a couple of large bass, and two or
three good-sized catfish. The small fish, of course, escape through
the holes of the smaller meshed net. The use of trammel nets

and seines is now illegal in most states, but in the late eighties Texas had comparatively few fish-and-game laws that we knew of in our community.

Sometimes my brother George and I would take a neighbor boy or two with us when we went fishing at Henrietta Creek. Upon one occasion John Clark was with us. It was a beautiful June day, and the water was clear as crystal. In many pools we could see bass sixteen to eighteen inches long; but though we dangled a hook baited with worms, grasshoppers, crickets, or a small frog directly in front of them they showed no interest in any kind of bait we might offer.

As we walked along the creek bank we came to a large deep pool of water with a long narrow inlet stretching away sixty to seventy feet to the southwest. Near the upper end of this we saw a beautiful bass at least eighteen inches long apparently sunning himself in the shallow water. George whispered softly to John and me, "Boys, you stand here and stop him from getting back into the main creek. I'll slip up and dangle this big grasshopper on my hook right in front of him. Now turn him back if he starts for deep water." John was standing on the bank of the inlet and I was a yard or so below him. We both hardly breathed as George sneaked very cautiously to a point well back of the bank and gently tossed his hook into the water.

Evidently the fish saw his shadow and was gone like an arrow. Turn him back! We might as well have tried to turn back a flash of lightning! John jumped into the middle of the inlet with a mightly splash, but before he hit the water the fish was far below and in the deep pool. John came out looking a little foolish and pretty wet, for the clear water was a good deal deeper than it looked. He dried out quickly, however, in the hot sun.

We fished all day and caught nothing but a few small bream and perch until late in the afternoon when we were all fishing in a big deep pool. George's cork suddenly plunged under and he landed a channel cat at least eighteen inches long. While George was removing the hook John rushed up and, standing almost in George's tracks, threw his hook into the water at as nearly as possible the exact spot where the fish had been caught. Evidently he thought that fish came in pairs like shoes. He fished diligently there for fifteen minutes but not a nibble rewarded his efforts.

The sun was nearly down by this time, and we had three miles to walk. We reluctantly wound our lines around the end of our fishing poles, pushed the sharp end of the hook into the cork, and started for home. It had been a happy day even if we had caught but few fish. George was very proud of his big channel cat, which is one of the most delicious fish to be found in the streams of Texas or any other state.

During the summer that my brother John and his wife lived with us my father took me with him on a fishing trip to Henrietta Creek. For some reason George and the rest of the family did not go, probably because they were eager to finish some job on the farm. Father and I went in the spring wagon, took a lunch with us, and spent the day. On this trip my father proved that he was not idly boasting when he claimed to be a superior fisherman. I managed to catch a fairly good string of perch; but he caught two black bass, one of them weighing over three pounds and the other slightly over four.

While we never felt that fishing was quite as much fun as

hunting, we were ardent anglers just the same, always ready to go fishing when the opportunity was offered us. Moreover, we rejoiced as much when we caught a long string of fish as we did over a successful hunt. Our method of fishing with a cork or bobber which had to be watched closely may have increased our powers of concentration. At any rate, when I went to bed at night after fishing half a day, the moment my eyes were closed I could see my cork on the water bobbing a little at times as a perch or catfish nibbled at the bait.

Perhaps it is not surprising that most people of the Cross Timbers had some superstitions as to fish and fishing. Apparently most persons today are not entirely free of such superstitions. Fish seem to bite or not bite "without rhyme or reason." Sometimes one may find the fishing good one day and the following day never get a nibble at the same spot using the same bait. Occasionally fish may take the bait ravenously for an hour or so and then mysteriously stop biting.

Scientists may provide the answers, but the average person fishes in the realm of metaphysics! He has no idea what causes him to have "good luck" one day and "no luck" at all the next; or why when three or four persons are fishing, one catches a dozen and the others catch only two or three. It is not surprising that "fisherman's luck" has become a stock phrase. Even today anyone passing a fisherman dangling his hook in the water never asks, "Are you catching many?" Always it is, "Having any luck?" or "What luck are you having?"

Not only did the age-old mystery which clings to the vocation of the Apostle Peter and Izaak Walton affect us in my boyhood but it seems to be nationwide, if not world-wide, even today. In addition, the "fringe benefits" of a fishing trip which we received as boys were not too unlike those that come to modern business or professional men who go fishing. We had a day or half day of freedom from work in the field, just as they can get away from the office and the petty details of their business.

I can still recall with great pleasure the long walks over the green, flower-spangled prairie to Henrietta Creek, with a big jack rabbit jumping up occasionally to go loping off, turning slightly sideways just to show that he was in no particular hurry. Once the stream was reached it was real luxury to sit on a rock in a shady spot beside a deep foam-flecked pool and watch your cork floating on the water, hoping any instant to see it plunge under. Even if only small ones were caught, or none at all for an hour or so, you knew that big ones were in there and sooner or later you would surely hook one.

When the sun indicated that it was about noon there was the lunch to unpack and eat. Bacon-and-egg sandwiches made with big slices of homemade bread, sweet sandwiches with butter and jam or jelly generously spread on the bread, and perhaps a few cookies or pieces of cake tasted much better when eaten while we were sitting on a rock beside a clear stream than they would at home.

No doubt the "tired business man" on a similar trip carrying a hundred dollars worth of equipment now feels as we boys of the Texas Cross Timbers did nearly three-quarters of a century ago—that going fishing is always fun regardless of whether you catch any fish or "have no luck" at all. Moreover, it has been said that "Providence does not deduct from one's life span the hours spent in fishing."

9. School and Schoolmates

My formal schooling began late. The school laws of Texas during the time we lived in the Cross Timbers provided free schools for all pupils from eight to sixteen years of age, inclusive. Compulsory education lay far in the future and it is doubtful if any proposal for a law compelling parents to send their children to school between specified ages would have received many votes, at least in our community.

Since I had learned to read long before I had reached free-school age, my father saw little reason to send me to school earlier or to keep me there the entire term if I was needed at home to thin corn, chop cotton, or do other useful work. George had attended school a little at Lone Star Schoolhouse when we lived on the rented farm on the prairie.

One day, several months after my mother's death, Alice took me with her to visit one of her friends in Keller, who lived near the two-room schoolhouse. When we saw the children playing at afternoon recess, she asked me if I would like to go to the school playground, sit with George during the final period, and come home with him. Of course I was thrilled at the prospect of visiting a schoolroom and ran over to the playground as fast as my little legs could carry me.

A game of ball was going on, but George seemed glad to see me. In a few minutes the bell rang, and all the youngsters trooped into their respective rooms, the small fry to the "little room" and the larger ones to the "big room." I tagged right along with George, who was in the so-called "big room" presided over by "Professor" Moore, while the teacher of the smaller kids was Miss Jennie Curtis. A man teaching, even in a one-room school, was always called "professor," while the pupils were called "scholars," a gross overstatement of fact, but hardly more so than referring to *all* young persons in college as "students"!

I sat down by George, who had a double desk but no deskmate, and gazed with wondering eyes at my strange surroundings, for this was my first time inside a schoolroom. The blackboard, the raised platform on which Professor Moore's desk stood, the erasers hanging by long strings from nails just above the blackboard, and the mottoes on the wall all fascinated me. I noticed too that the girls all sat on the south side of the room and the boys on the north side, that a big wood stove stood in the center of the room to supply heat.

The first class called was in algebra and had only three or four of the biggest boys in school. One of them, Albert Hussey, was called upon to solve a problem. He wrote some strange symbols on the blackboard, combined them with large letters of the alphabet and figures, and at last took a long stick, which I later learned was called a pointer, and pointing it at the various letters and symbols began to speak with a strong nasal voice, "Now, if *A* eenqual *B* and *B* eenqual *C*, then *A* eenquals *C*." I looked and listened goggle-eyed, as I said to myself, "Gee whiz, how does

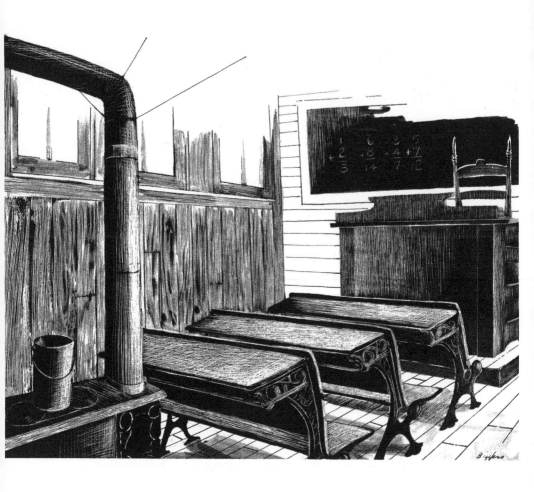

he know that?" Such wisdom was far beyond by understanding!

The algebra class was at last dismissed and returned to the seats its members had originally occupied. Then a class in grammar was called, and a dozen boys and girls arose and moved forward to sit on the two long benches directly in front of the platform on which stood the Professor's desk.

Half of them were sent to the blackboard and Professor Moore read from a book a sentence to each member of the group to be written on the board. I could read the sentences fairly easily;

but when the teacher asked the pupils to "diagram the sentence" and they began by drawing long lines on which some of the words were written and from them drew slanting or broken lines on which other words of the sentence were written, I despaired of understanding what was going on and lost all interest in the subsequent proceedings. Apparently George did not have a class in the period following afternoon recess and could devote the entire time to studying his lessons for the next day.

The grammar class was followed by one in geography, which interested me a great deal. Then came one in physiology, which was also of considerable interest. Finally, at about ten minutes to four, when school was to be dismissed, or "let out," or "turned out," in the idiom of the Cross Timbers, came roll call.

As the teacher called the roll, in which names were in alphabetical order, a pupil who had reached school on time and had not whispered to any schoolmate during the day answered, "Perfect." If he had been late, his answer was, "Tardy"; if he had whispered without permission it was, "Imperfect."

Then two of the older students each passed a small tray of little cards bearing the words *One Token of Merit.* Everyone who had been "Perfect" took one. George had told me that when you got five of these you exchanged them for a larger five-tokens-of-merit card, and that fifty tokens of merit brought you a large and very beautiful colored card.

When I was about seven and a half years old my father decided to start me to school. It happened to be near the end of the month and when my first week of school ended, Father received a bill for my tuition as I was under the free-school age. Because it seemed to him unreasonably large, after he had paid it he de-

cided that it would be just as well for me to study at home until
I was eight years old.

Study at home was not too bad. George's school books I had
already gone over with special interest. In his McGuffey's readers,
I had already memorized most of the poems. Also, his big geography and physiology textbooks had proved to be very interesting.

I now began to study the more difficult words in Webster's
Blueback Speller. Alice would assign my lessons and after one
had been studied for an hour or so, she would take the book
and pronounce, or "give out," the words to me; it was unusual
for me to miss one. Arithmetic was very difficult for me and
though I studied the multiplication table diligently and prac-
ticed "doing sums" in addition, subtraction, and multiplication
with some regularity, my knowledge of arithmetic, penmanship,
and English usage lagged far behind that of reading, spelling,
geography, and history.

When my eighth birthday came in February, 1887, it was so
late in the term that it seemed useless for me to enter school until
autumn. Fairly early in the fall of 1887, however, I entered the
Keller School and was placed in the "little room." Miss Julia
Leverett was the teacher and her brother, "Professor" Leverett,
presided over the other room and taught the older students. So
many big girls and boys attended school, however, that Miss Julia
heard two classes coming in from his room each day—one in
advanced arithmetic and the other in grammar.

The Leveretts were from Arkansas, and evidently Mr. Leverett
had at some time attended a military school or perhaps had received military training in college. At any rate, he quickly

organized all of the bigger boys into a company and gave them half-an-hour's drill after school and usually drilled them another half hour during the noon intermission.

This was something entirely new to the students of the Keller School and some of their parents were a trifle skeptical as to the value of such drills, but the boys seemed to like them. The older girls also appeared to be fascinated by the activities of the marching column of boys as they obeyed such commands as: "fall in, right-dress, front, forward, common-time march, right, left, right, left, halt, column right—march."

Miss Julia seemed to be a good teacher. Her pupils sat on long benches with a long slightly sloping board in front of them, on which the kids rested their slates and tablets when writing. As there were no closets in which to hang hats and caps, they were usually on this long desk in front of the pupils. When the older students came in from the other room for their arithmetic lesson one of them would often pick up some small boy's hat and start using it as an eraser if Miss Julia's back was turned.

The small youngster upon seeing his precious little wool headgear so mistreated would lift his hand high in the air, wave it frantically to and fro, and start snapping his fingers. As Miss Julia, who had put a ban on finger snapping, started to turn around, the hat would be tossed back in front of its owner. Seeking to justify himself the small lad would exclaim, "John Merrill was a-racin' with my hat!" The only result was that he was reprimanded for snapping his fingers, while the real culprit got off scot free!

At the end of a couple of weeks Miss Julia gave an examination to the fourth-reader class, in which I had been placed, to see if some of the members might not be advanced to the fifth-reader group, which sat in the other room. After all of us had read aloud a few paragraphs containing some fairly difficult words, two or three were advanced to the fifth reader and sent to Mr. Leverett's room. Miss Julia told me that my reading was as good as the best of these but because of my youth and lack of knowledge of arithmetic she thought it best for me to stay in her room until after Christmas. After the holidays were over, however, I was sent to Mr. Leverett's room to join the fifth-reader class.

The country kids, who constituted the great majority of the pupils, all walked to school carrying their lunches in a tin-covered pail called a "dinner bucket." As indicated in an earlier chapter, the people of the Cross Timbers always called the midday meal dinner and the evening meal supper. Also, the word "pail" was completely alien to their speech. Always it was a water bucket, milk bucket, and dinner bucket.

The contents of the dinner buckets varied widely, usually consisting of sandwiches made of large biscuits cut in halves and buttered, with a couple of slices of bacon or a fried egg between the two halves. Sometimes the filling might be a slice of ham or a cake of sausage. Instead of an egg sandwich there might be a couple of boiled eggs. Usually included were some cookies or a piece of cake, pie, gingerbread, or a fried pie. In some cases there might be a teacup half-full of sorghum or a bottle of milk. Generally, the bucket contained plenty of solid, substantial food calculated to "stick to the ribs" throughout a long day, though a modern dietitian would probably hold up her hands in horror at such food for growing children!

It was a mile-and-a-half walk from our house to Keller and the schoolhouse was just beyond the east edge of the village. We usually walked down the road along the south edge of our lower field to the railroad and followed it to town, which we had to cross to reach the school. Some boys, including Sumter and Hubert Boone and Bill Mayes had to walk farther than George and I did, so that we usually had company on the way to and from school.

The usual perennial feud existed between the town and country boys, and small fights were fairly common. Under the "common law" of most rural and village schools all pupils were responsible to the teacher while on the way home. Moreover, in the Keller School the youngsters were expected to go directly home, and any country kid who lingered unduly long in town was likely to be called before Mr. Leverett and asked to explain why.

I recall that one day when George and I had started home and had got as far as town, we found Father there with the wagon loading up some groceries; we stopped and waited until he was ready to go home. Oscar McCain, whose home was on the road about halfway between town and our place, waited to ride with us.

Unfortunately, Mr. Leverett saw us as he was going home, and the next morning soon after school opened called, "George Dale, Ed Dale, and Oscar McCain come front." As this was only about a week after my promotion to his room, I froze with horror but rose and followed George and Oscar up to the teacher's desk with my knees shaking a little. "George," said Mr. Leverett, "why were you fooling around town last evening after school?"

"Well sir," George began, "Paw was there with the wagon
and . . ."

"Oh, you and your brother were waiting for a ride home.
Oscar, how about you?"

"Well, Mr. Dale was there with the wagon and goes right by
our house . . ."

"I see. You were waiting for a ride too. All right. Seats, pass."

This was my only time in school to be "called up on the
carpet," although probably not the only time I *should* have been
called. Always there were some boys less fortunate, although no
school I ever attended had more than one or two tough lads in it
and none of these ever gave the teacher any serious trouble. Since
drill largely took the place of playing games for the older boys,
little playing was done at recess or during the noon hour except
by the smaller boys and little girls. The big girls got enough entertainment by watching the larger boys drill!

Just what was the length of the Keller term of school, I'm
not sure. Picking cotton in the fall always forced me to enter
school late, and thinning corn and chopping cotton made it
necessary for me to quit early in the spring. In consequence, it is
doubtful if my attendance was ever more than five or six months
of any term and was probably less.

As noted in a previous chapter, Alice and I left the Cross
Timbers home for Navajoe in Greer County in October, 1888,
to be followed by Father and George a month or so later. As
earlier stated my four or five months of schooling in that little
frontier town did much to advance my education. This was not
because Miss Anna was an outstanding teacher, for she was not.
It was due to the fact that she lent me so many good books, which

I devoured at a most impressionable age. Up to that time I had been starved for reading matter, and every book was a feast.

As George remained in Greer County only about three months, he did not enter school that year. Moreover, neither of us had any schooling to amount to anything the following year, 1889–1890. By the time we had spent a month or more in camp on Walnut Creek picking cotton, had returned to help Tom for a few weeks, and at last had regained possession of our home, it was close to midwinter. With the school term nearly half over and so much work to do in repairing fences and making other improvements which our old tenant had neglected, we were needed to work on the farm.

Moreover, since we did not have Alice to cook and keep house we were keeping "bachelor's hall," and did our own cooking and housekeeping. Eventually we worked out a fairly good division of labor. Father milked the cows, George did most of the housework, and I did the lion's share of the cooking during the crop season, although Father often cooked breakfast. During the winter months when I was in school Father did most of the cooking. Dish washing was usually my job even when I was attending school, except at noon of course during the five days of school each week.

Unlike the school year of 1889–1890, I attended the Keller School regularly the following year for the entire term of seven months. The Leveretts had gone and the teacher in the big room was Professor Minor, while the small youngsters were taught by a young woman from one of the nearby towns.

Mr. Minor introduced us to what he called the Rugby type of football. It was played with a big round ball about the size of a basketball. Two goal posts were set up at each end of the field, which was about the length of a modern football field. The objective was to drive the ball between the two goal posts with the feet. The ball could not be touched by the hand except when it was in the air.

We developed a great enthusiasm for the game and played it not only at school but at home when four or five boys got together. We had no real football of course except at school, but an ordinary yarn ball was a fairly satisfactory substitute. The game was hard on shoes and harder still on shins at times, but it was great fun.

We sat at double desks and my deskmate, a little older than myself, was Willie Mulkey, an orphan, who lived with his aunt. Before a month of school had gone by Willie had developed a great crush on Lela Ponder, a little tow-headed girl about twelve years old, whose desk was on the south side of the room almost directly opposite ours.

Lela, always called "Lelar" in the vernacular of the Cross Timbers, apparently reciprocated Willie's affection; but the girls' playground was on the south and west sides of the schoolhouse and that of the boys' on the east and north sides. Moreover, the girls' playground was strictly off limits for boys. The young Romeo had almost no opportunity to talk with his Juliet, for they lived in opposite directions from the schoolhouse and could not walk home together.

In desperation Willie took the only means of communication open to him—writing surreptitious notes. How long this clandestine correspondence had been going on I never knew, for my deskmate must have been very discreet in getting his notes delivered.

One day, however, when the teacher's back was turned, Willie undertook to slip a note across to his beloved; but Mr. Minor suddenly turned and caught him in the act.

"Willie," Professor Minor said kindly, "I am sure we would all be interested in anything you write. Will you please stand and read that to us."

Willie began to cry but Mr. Minor's voice grew stern as he said, "Come on Willie, stand up and read it to us. We are all waiting."

Willie staggered to his feet, stifled his sobs, and in a shaky but distinct voice read his epistle, "My Dear Lelar, I thought I would write you a few lines to let you know that I am well. Did you get the big apple I gave the other girl to give you? Lovingly yours, Willie." As he finished reading he sat down, folded his arms on the desk, and dropped his face on them as he wept silently.

"That is very good Willie," said the teacher gently. "She knows you're well now, so you can get back to work."

Willie sat up in a minute or two. His grief had been replaced by furious anger; and behind the big geography book, which was the text for our next class, he poured into my unwilling ears a whispered, bitter monologue consisting mostly of dire threats of vengeance.

"I'll git eben with him," he declared violently. "I'll git eben with him if it takes all this year. I wouldn't be surprised if I come up here some night and cut all of them herasers down. Maybe I'll bring some molasses up here some night and pour it all over the top of his desk or put some long sharp tacks in his chair. Maybe next spring I might ketch a snake and put in his desk. Makin' me read that note! I'll git eben with him some way." Willie was merely letting off steam in whispering to me all the things he was going to do to "git eben" with Mr. Minor. He doubtless got much pleasure out of this, but as a matter of fact he never did anything.

This was by far the longest term I attended during my years in the Cross Timbers. Mr. Minor was an inspiring teacher and for me there was never a dull moment during any school day. He put new mottoes up on the wall, such as "Education is Wealth," "Knowledge is Power," and several others. In addition, he often stayed after school to write wise sayings of literary men on the board and asked us to look up others to give at roll call. Those who did not find some new quotations might read one from those on the wall or those written on the blackboard.

Although this was done only about once or twice a month, most of the so-called "scholars" did not bother to look up a special quotation but read one from wall or board. A few of us, however, always had something ready to give when the roll was called. They varied from, "I only regret that I have but one life to give for my country" or "God tempers the wind to the shorn lamb" to "One must eat to live, and not live to eat."

As in most other schools of that time the period after Friday afternoon recess was usually given over to "speaking pieces" or a spelling match, although we occasionally had a "ciphering match." This was the period when we often had a few visitors, which put everyone on his mettle. The speeches were often taken from one of McGuffey's readers, although we were not using them but a new series. Included in the recitations were familiar old poems or in some instances a prose selection.

In the spelling matches the teacher usually asked an older boy and girl to serve as captains. As it would have been neither dignified nor practical to use the "wet-or-dry" method of deciding who had first choice, the teacher held up a book, stated how many pages it had, and slipped a finger between the leaves not far from the middle. The captain whose guess was closest to the page number where the finger held the book open had first choice. The one chosen arose and stood beside the captain. In this way choosing went back and forth until all pupils stood in two long lines facing each other.

The teacher then pronounced the words from the spelling book, starting with fairly easy ones in order to give the poorer spellers a chance to stand in line for a few minutes at least. When one missed spelling a word he returned to his seat. This was continued sometimes until only one on each side was left to carry on a duel and until one of them went down and the other won a victory for his side.

This was called "spelling down the school." It was my good fortune to win this honor a number of times. In addition, my love for poetry usually enabled me to make a fairly creditable showing in speaking. In a "ciphering match," however, my weakness was readily apparent and no captain chose me early in the game. It must be admitted that in either spelling or arithmetic the competition was not too keen.

During this term of school a new set of readers had been adopted. This pleased me, for although I had always used McGuffey's readers and had a great respect for them, it was good to have a new fifth reader, as I was still in the fifth-reader class. The new book had many new poems and prose articles.

Yet, McGuffey's fourth, fifth, and sixth readers did much to advance my education. They gave me at least some acquaintance with many of the authors in the fields of English and American literature up to that time. In them were found extracts from the writings of Shakespeare, Dickens, Scott, Southey, Tennyson, Byron, Goldsmith, Wordsworth, Gray, Hood, Bryant, Longfellow, Poe, Irving, Whittier, Everett, Beecher, and many others.

All of these I read and reread at a most impressionable age and memorized many of the poems and quite a few passages from some of the prose selections. As a result, such characters as Falstaff, Prince Hal, Shylock, Brutus, Mark Antony, Cassius, Little Nell, young Lochinvar, Robert Bruce, the Disinherited Knight, David Copperfield, Hiawatha, Miles Standish, Paul Revere, Rip Van Winkle, the Village Blacksmith, and a host of others became as real to me as were my own playmates or their fathers. It is true that I did not understand everything and frequently called upon George to explain a stanza or paragraph, which he never failed to do.

After I had memorized "Paul Revere's Ride," George was asked to explain the meaning of one stanza:

> A hurry of hoofs in the village street
> A shape in the moonlight, a bulk in the dark
> And beneath from the pebbles in passing a spark
> Struck out by a steed flying fearless and fleet
> That was all, and yet through the gloom and the light
> The fate of a nation was riding that night
> And the spark struck out by that steed in his flight
> Kindled the land into flame with its heat.

"Just what does that mean, George?" I asked.

"Mean?" replied George. "It means just what it says. You've seen sparks fly when we'd hit a rock a glancing lick with a hammer. Well, ole Paul's horse was shod, so his iron shoes knocked sparks from rocks and set the whole blamed country a-fire. You know the leaves and grass would still be dry in April that far north. Why before we had matches, people always had to use a flint and steel to start a fire."

Of course I accepted this explanation as I did everything else that my big brother told me. Sparks from coal-burning locomotives often set the dry leaves on fire during the winter season in our neighborhood. In fact, such fires had burned part of our brush fences and made it necessary to split more rails to enclose one side of a field.

Mr. Minor's school was the last one that I attended long enough to amount to anything during my ten years of life in the Cross Timbers. The following year, 1891–1892, a new man came to teach the Keller School. Rains delayed cotton picking that autumn so that we were late getting ours picked and then we also helped some of the neighbors. In consequence, the school term was half over before I entered. As spring planting caused me to leave early, my attendance that year was only for a few weeks.

During the few years that I was of school age it is doubtful if I attended the Keller School as much as twelve months. Certainly, I learned more at home by reading during these years than at school. In fact, only at Mr. Minor's school did I feel that my education was advanced very much. Most of the other teachers declared that review was useful and put me back in all subjects to go over material that I had studied the previous year.

Yet, my schooling in these years was not without its rewards. I became familiar with classroom procedure, picked up much information from the reading of pupils in the more advanced classes, and made many new friends. During the long walks to and from school I developed close friendships with two or three other boys, with whom I later visited and played.

10. Cross Timbers Society

For older people of the Cross Timbers, social activities or diversions were limited largely to all-day visits, such as we often had with the Brileys, short visits in the afternoon or evening with nearby neighbors, and attendance at Church and Sunday School. Since my father was a devout member of the Primitive Baptist Church, whose members did not believe in Sunday Schools, none of us ever attended the Sunday Schools of the Methodists or Missionary Baptists, which were the leading denominations at Keller.

The Primitive, or Old School, Baptists, often called the "Hardshell Baptists," are usually depicted as a grossly ignorant group who practice foot washing and oppose not only Sunday Schools but foreign missions. No doubt, many Hardshell Baptists in the mountainous regions of some of the states farther east are backward and ignorant even today, but this was not true of the group to which my father belonged.

Among the leading members of his church was Brother McKelvey, a Civil War veteran from Tennessee, who was for several years county treasurer of Denton County. Others were Brother McMakin of Georgia, who took the *Atlanta Constitution* and believed implicitly everything he read in it. Still others were prosperous farmers, including Brother Bourland, who lived only about a mile southeast of our home in one of the largest and most attractive houses in the community.

Although he did not believe in Sunday Schools, our father's Church meant everything to him. He was never happier than when some of his "brethren" came to visit us or when he could visit some of them, and the weather was never too severe for him to attend church. For several years the nearest church of his faith was the Denton Creek Church, some ten miles from our home, but a year or so before we left the Cross Timbers a church was built at Keller. This pleased Father very much, for then we could entertain in our home some of his Church brothers who lived several miles away.

George and I always shook hands with such visitors and called them "Brother" McMakin or "Brother" Howard instead of "Mister." We thoroughly enjoyed their visits even when we were keeping "bachelor's hall" and did our best to help provide them with well-cooked and tasty meals. We enjoyed their conversations too, for although they talked of religion and the Bible a great deal, they frequently told of their old home lands and their boyhood days.

Brother McKelvey was an especially entertaining talker. He had served for the four years of the Civil War in the Confederate army. During these years he had participated in many battles and bore the scars of many wounds.

"When I enlisted in the Southern army soon after the war started," he once told us, "I thought that to get shot meant to be killed, but after being wounded half a dozen times, I learned that this was not true."

He said he was so badly wounded in one battle that he was sent to the "dead house" along with the dead and dying, while the surgeons gave their attention to the wounded that they could save or that they had some hope of saving. After lying all night among the dead bodies of his comrades, he was still living in the morning when the detail came to bury the dead. He was then removed to a field hospital and within a couple of months was back with his regiment again.

Such stories made Brother McKelvey a doubly welcome guest, but he also related humorous incidents of his life as a boy and youth in Tennessee. Some of these stories dealt with social events such as candy pullings and expeditions to pick up hickory nuts or gather wild grapes or pawpaws. These stories were always told with rare humor and in a most interesting fashion. Many other members of our father's church who visited us told stirring tales of their adventures as boys or young men before coming to Texas.

While Father and other members of his church derived a great deal of pleasure from church going, the fact that there were no Sunday Schools, prayer meetings, or ladies'-aid societies made the Old School Baptist Church somewhat less important as a social institution than were the other churches, which had such features, as well as an Epworth League, Christian Endeavor, or Baptist Young People's Union.

In addition to participating in church activities and all-day Sunday visits, older women often met in groups to do quilting and to piece quilts, or in a sewing circle to visit while they worked at patching their husbands' and children's clothing, at knitting socks, sewing on buttons, and making dresses or other clothing for themselves and their children.

Such meetings were always in the afternoon and the women's

tongues often moved faster than their fingers as they discussed the local news and gossip. In the summer they often brought their smaller children, who played outside—the little girls making play houses and the small boys riding stick horses around the yard or playing some simple game such as marbles or "last-one-on-wood-is-a-bear."

The older men sometimes found the grocery store an attractive social center. This was especially true in winter, when they could sit around the big potbellied stove, chew tobacco, and spit in a flat tobacco box, which was full of sand. Here was an ideal place for the cross-pollination of ideas on politics, religion, and local affairs. The gristmill on Bear Creek, a mile or more east of Keller, was an equally good place for such "man-talk" while waiting to get a "turn" of corn ground.

As for society in the usual sense of the word, meaning socials, dances, parties, dinners, and luncheons, I was only a more-or-less disinterested observer. Kid parties may have been given in the larger towns or cities, but in rural communities such as ours they were unknown. When a boy had a birthday he was lucky if his mother baked him a cake and only one or two persons spanked him, giving him one lick for each year of his life and "one to grow on."

As I was only thirteen when we left the Cross Timbers, girls played little or no part in my life there. Of course, Minnie Brown, referred to in an earlier chapter, was a good playmate, and I liked her, but my feeling about girls was that of the average small boy, who regards them as an unmitigated nuisance. I admitted that there might be an occasional exception but not many.

Of course, George would often tease me about girls even when I was very small, usually choosing some little girl in the neighborhood that he knew I detested, such as Jane Blodgett or Effie Clark. As a boy I had the devil's own temper, and if something happened to make me angry when I was playing with other children some little girl was sure to chant the old verse:

> Ed is mad and I am glad
> But I know what would please him.
> A bottle of wine to make him shine
> And Effie Clark to squeeze him.

This, of course, made me doubly furious, but I could do nothing about it except grind my teeth and say to myself, "Oh, if you were only a boy!"

In previous chapters it has been shown that my brother George was my "guide, philosopher and friend" throughout my boyhood years. Always he was to me the fountainhead of all wisdom, and anything he told me was accepted as Gospel truth. We had never been separated for a single day until Alice and I went west to Navajoe, and when Father and I started on the return journey in June, 1899, my most cherished thought was of being with George again.

When at long last we reached the home of Tom and Lucy, and George came out to meet us, it was hard to restrain my joy. He seemed equally glad to see me, for it had been three or four months since he had left Navajoe to return to the Cross Timbers and help Tom make a crop.

Of course we had many things to talk about, but I could not avoid feeling a little disappointed when I discovered that George had a girl! It was not jealousy exactly, but a realization that we no longer had identical interests. Up to that time the current of our thoughts and actions had always run in a common channel— work, playing games with other boys or with one another, fishing, hunting, telling stories, reading and talking over what we had read, plus rambling in the woods in search of mulberries, wild grapes, plums, and persimmons. Now George had an important interest which I could not share.

Obviously, I should not have been surprised. George was now about sixteen and for several months had been living with Tom and Lucy, whose home was always a haven for young people. Lucy was the youngest child in a family of five children. She had married Tom when she was only a kid not quite sixteen and had never entirely grown up.

For eight years after her marriage she had no children, and with her husband at work in the fields all day she would have been very lonely had she not always had some girl or woman in her home most of the time. They were not hired girls, but guests, although they always helped with the dishes and other house-work. There was little to do, for Lucy was a notoriously sloppy housekeeper, but she was an excellent cook, and she could always find some girl or woman glad to come and stay for several weeks in return for good meals and lodging.

Because Lucy dearly loved young people and was a born match-maker there were few Sunday afternoons that two or three young couples did not drop in, sure of a cordial welcome and refreshments of lemonade and cookies, cake, or gingerbread. She was always willing to give a party, at which the young people played such "parlor" games as "pussy wants a corner," "blind man's buff," "fruit basket," or some of the play-party games.

Dancing was regarded as sinful in our part of the Cross Tim-bers, where most of the older people were members of either the Methodist or Baptist Church. There was apparently no objection, however, to the play-party games, in which singing took the place of music. The term "music" is used with reservations, for by no stretch of the imagination could the singing of most of the play-ers be called "vocal music."

The origin of some of these games is obscure, but no doubt

most of them had been brought to the Texas Cross Timbers as part of the cultural baggage of immigrants from Tennessee, North Carolina, Arkansas, and other Southern states.

Among these many games were "Skip to My Lou," previously mentioned as a game that Uncle Jack Clark had played in Tennessee, and "Little Brass Wagon," closely resembling the Virginia Reel. Still others were "Old Dan Tucker," "The Miller Boy," "Hog Drovers," "Coffee Grows on White Oak Trees," "Mr. Buster," "We're Marching Down to New Orleans," "Buffalo Girls," and many more.

The tunes were often quite catchy, but the words meant very little and were sometimes sheer drivel, as may be seen by the first stanza of some that were most popular in our community:

> We're marching down to New Orleans
> With our drums and fifes a-beating
> The Americans are gaining of the day
> And the British are retreating.

> Mr. Buster, do you love sugar in tea
> Mr. Buster, do you love candy
> Mr. Buster, he can reel and turn
> And swing those girls so handy.

> Happy is the miller boy that lives by the mill
> The mill turns around with a free good will.
> One hand on the hopper and the other in the sack
> The ladies step forward and the gents step back.

There were variations in the words of "The Miller Boy," but in both it and "Old Dan Tucker," there was an extra man, who tried to steal a partner when the ladies stepped forward and the gents stepped back .

In "Old Dan Tucker" the words were as follows:

> Old Dan Tucker's down in town
> A-swinging the ladies all around
> First to the right and then to the left
> Then the one he loves the best.
>
> Get out of the way for Old Dan Tucker
> Came too late to get his supper.
> Supper is over and nothin a-cookin,
> And Old Dan Tucker stands there lookin'
> Dance Tucker, dance Tucker.

The game was played by the couples standing in a circle, while the extra boy, who represented Old Dan Tucker, stood in the middle. After each boy had swung the girl to his right and the one to his left and the "one he loved the best," with the words, "Get out of the way for Old Dan Tucker," the boy and girl of each couple faced each other, joined hands, and danced with short sideways steps completely around the circle in what was called "promenading."

The objective of Old Dan Tucker was to steal the partner of some boy who had left her side for a moment to "swing the one he loved the best." If he succeeded the man left without a partner became the next Dan Tucker. In any case, however, the lone man was expected to dance a brief jig as the couples chanted "Dance Tucker" while they rested a moment from their promenade.

While this was one of the simplest of the play-party games, none of them were as complex as are some of the square-dance figures of today. I never attended any of the play parties, but when Lucy had a group of young people in for an evening I often joined in in such simple games as "blindfold," "pinning the tail on the donkey," and in summer such outdoor games as "drop the handkerchief," in which both boys and girls took part. George did not go to as many such parties as some boys of the community but went at times and knew all the songs. George's romance with this first girl was also brief, but there were others later.

The school at Keller was never a social center except that older people sometimes visited it on Friday afternoons when we had "speaking pieces" or spelling or arithmetic matches. In contrast, the one-room rural school called Mount Gilead, only two or three miles east of our home, had a flourishing literary society every year, which met twice a month on Friday evenings. Not only most of the pupils took part but also many young people of the community who were not in school.

George and I attended its meetings a few times but never appeared on the programs, which consisted of recitations and declamations, drills, and similar activities by the small fry, and one-act plays by the older persons. The recitations and declamations included such old favorites as "Curfew Must Not Ring Tonight," "How We Tried to Lick the Teacher," "The Widder Spriggins' Daughter," "Spartacus to the Gladiators," and "The Face on the Bar Room Floor."

The younger children, of course, gave short and simple poems and sometimes put on a stunt, in which several small youngsters took part. One, for example, was called "Choice of Trades." In this, a half dozen small boys, each dressed in suitable garb for his future vocation and carrying the appropriate tools, appeared one by one and recited a short stanza of verse. The lad hoping to study medicine came out with a doctor's bag and gave a brief speech:

When I am a man, a man as you see
I'll be a doctor if I can, and I can.
My pills and powders will be nice and sweet
And you may have just what you want to eat
When I am a man.

He might be followed by a would-be farmer wearing a blue shirt and overalls with a hoe or rake over his shoulder. He gave his little speech and retired to be followed by a future cowboy, carpenter, painter, teacher, lawyer. Then they all appeared and marched across the stage, each reciting his own verse.

The young men and women who were not in school usually gave one-act plays called dialogues. These included such favorites as *The Train to Mauro, Arabella's Poor Relations,* and *Marrying a Poetess.* Others might be blackface comedies, in which some of the characters blacked their faces with burnt cork for their roles as Negroes. The meetings of the Mount Gilead Literary Society were interesting, and the schoolhouse was always filled to overflowing.

The summer months were usually marked by a huge Fourth of July picnic, and often two or three smaller picnics were held by some Sunday School. Fireworks did not seem to have as much prominence on the Fourth of July as they had at Christmas. Thanksgiving was seldom celebrated at all, at least in our community, and comparatively little attention was given to Easter except by a few families that colored eggs for the children.

A Fourth of July picnic, however, brought out almost everyone in our neighborhood, for there was always at least one lemonade stand, from which the proprietor loudly proclaimed, "Ice-cold lemonade, made in the shade and stirred with a spade, milk shake

and sody-pop!" The youngsters patronized it freely if they had
any money. The lemonade was usually in a large barrel which,
like the legendary miraculous pitcher, never became dry, for the
proprietor added water and ice from time to time. As a result, by
the late afternoon the lemon rinds floating on top and a strong
imagination were required to assure the patron that he was actually drinking lemonade.

In addition to the cold-drinks stand there was always a merry-
go-round. The power for running this was furnished by a de-
jected-looking mule, whose appearance indicated that he could
see little point in walking slowly around and around the central
post all day with only slight pauses when the merry-go-round
stopped to let some of its passengers off and to take on others.
Often the owner and operator would give a seat to a couple of
musicians, who played a violin and an accordion and sometimes
sang as they whirled about. Sometimes there were other so-called
"attractions" as a doll rack or shooting gallery, but the cold-
drinks stand and merry-go-round were always present at large
picnics.

It is difficult to say whether the social behavior of the people
of the Texas Cross Timbers, between 1882 and 1892, differed
much from that of the rural inhabitants of other states in the
same period of time. Certainly great changes in our social customs
as a whole have occurred in the past three-quarters of a century.
It seems to me, however, that probably the Texas Cross Timbers
dwellers were at least slightly more Victorian in social behavior
than were those of the northern prairie states and possibly even
of some of the southern states.

Children were taught to say "yes sir" and "no sir" and "yes ma'am" and "no ma'am" to older persons. At the table children said "thank you for the bread" and "no thank you, I wouldn't choose [or wish] any" when refusing a dish of food passed to them. Napkins were almost unknown, and all members of a family used a common towel, comb, and brush, but a clean towel was given to guests.

No one except her husband, close relatives, and friends who had known her since girlhood ever called a married woman by her given name. Moreover, when a young man was introduced to Miss Mary Brown, for example, he called her "Miss Brown" for a long time before venturing to say "Miss Mary," and only after she had become a close friend did he call her "Mary."

Perhaps it was in their ideas concerning dress and speech that the Cross Timbers people of three-quarters of a century ago differed most from people of today. A calico dress and sunbonnet were worn by most women for everyday, while men wore a hickory shirt and either jeans pants or overalls. For Sunday the women wore hats to church, and men favored a blue serge suit and white shirt. Women's dresses, in any case, reached within an inch or two of the floor.

Little girls wore short skirts, and boys sometimes wore dresses until they were two or three years old. They were then given short pants or knickers and often did not put on long pants until they were eight or nine years old. Boys and girls went barefoot from about May until October, and they usually drove their parents nearly frantic by urging to be allowed to start going barefoot earlier than their elders thought was wise.

Young women wore hoops and bustles at one period, although the fashion did not last in our community, at least, longer than two or three years. Any woman who rode horseback used a side-saddle and wore a long black riding skirt. All men and boys wore a hat or cap when outside, and to remind a small boy to take off his hat when he came into the house was one of the minor crosses which most mothers had to bear.

A majority of the men of the Cross Timbers chewed tobacco, as did a considerable number of teen-age boys and some who had not reached their "teens." A few men smoked a pipe, but cigarette smoking was confined largely to older boys or young men, who usually rolled their own.

A great many women dipped snuff, but the only woman that I ever saw smoke was Grandma Gray, a very old lady who was blind. She lived with her son for many years, but after his death her more distant relatives decided to send her to the county poor-house. Because she quite naturally did not want to go there the members of my father's church agreed to keep her in their homes as long as she lived.

She came to us first for about two months. She smoked a clay pipe and among my duties were lighting her pipe with a sul-phur match or a coal from the fireplace and leading her when she wanted to take a walk. She lived for only a few months after leaving us for the home of another member of the Old School Baptist Church.

Father never used tobacco in any form, nor did George or I; yet, we were sometimes offered a chew by boys about our own age. When drying peaches we would often peel very soft free-stones, take out the seeds, crush the pulp, and spread it out on a clean board to dry. Once it was dry we would press eight or ten sheets of this together and cut it into plugs and offer to each other a chew of "tobe."

Probably the speech of the Cross Timbers people did not differ much from that of most other Southern uplanders. Fire was called "fahr," James was usually pronounced "Jeems," help in some instances became "holp," and "et" replaced eat, ate, and have eaten. A young man often "carried" his horse to water, a cow to the pasture, and his girl to church. A woman did not break her leg but a "lower limb." In fact, with floor-length skirts and the use of the term "limb," it almost seemed that it was a social error for a woman to admit that she had legs!

Many words or expressions freely used today were considered highly improper in Cross Timbers Society during my boyhood days. To refer to an unmarried woman's future children was a grave social error.

Upon one occasion I was at Tom and Lucy's home when the sewing circle was meeting there. The seven or eight women, including Betty Vick, an eighteen-year-old daughter of one of them, were talking about how badly spoiled some children of the neighborhood were. In a moment's lull of the conversation Betty said earnestly, "I'll tell you right now if I ever have any . . ." she stopped suddenly, blushed, and continued, "nieces or nephews, they are not going to be spoiled!"

Such words as "belly," "bull," "boar," and "pregnant" were never used in mixed company. One day six-year-old Ted Hurst, who was standing before a window, called excitedly, "Oh mommie! Mr. Preston's old bull is comin' down the road!"

"Teddy," his mother replied reprovingly, "you should say 'male'."

Ted was quite mindful of his mother's words, for the following morning he was again standing before the window and suddenly called to his mother, "Oh mommie! Mr. Preston's old male bull is comin' down the road again!"

Victorian as were the manners and customs of the people of the Cross Timbers, their social life was far from being drab or monotonous. In a time and place where entertainment and recreation were not purchasable commodities, the adults made their own, just as the children made their own toys. Moreover, something one makes for himself is always more precious than something bought.

The fact that most persons worked hard made periods of leisure more dear. School, church, socials, play parties, literary societies, visiting with friends and neighbors, and picnics or fishing trips were all a part of the social life of our community. Finally, to any man, woman, or child who has worked hard all day the opportunity to relax for an hour or two with a good book or magazine is a greater joy than any social function.

11. The Lure of the West

After living for ten years in our little Cross Timbers home we left it in November, 1892, for a new home in the Prairie West. A number of incidents and events fostered this removal but perhaps the chief factor was our father's inborn restless spirit, which had led him to cross the Plains to California in 1850, to the Pikes Peak area in 1858, to Nebraska soon after the close of the Civil War, and from that state to Texas.

Unquestionably my father, like many other Americans, was a born pioneer. He had bought this fifty-six–acre tract of wooded land and by a little over ten years of hard labor had transformed it into a well-improved and productive little farm. Now that he had nothing more to do than keep up the improvements and maintain the fertility of the soil he was ready to leave for the Prairie West to develop another tract of land.

As for George and me, by the time I was five years old, the word "West" brought to both of us mental pictures of a mighty, mysterious land of romance and adventure, where would be found Indians, cowboys, buffalo, panthers, and other wild animals. To us it was an enchanted land of wide plains and high mountains, which we hoped we might someday see. Our imaginations were further stimulated by occasional visits of relatives from the Prairie West.

Among these was Uncle Isaac, my father's young brother, referred to in an earlier chapter as migrating with my father from
Missouri to Nebraska and, some years later, from Nebraska to
Texas. His family at that time consisted of a son about eighteen
years old and two daughters, one about twenty and the other
about fifteen or sixteen years of age.

Soon after reaching Texas the son died, probably of pneu-
monia. The youth was the apple of his father's eye and his death
almost broke the old man's heart. A few months later the older
daughter married a young wheat farmer, who lived only a few
miles east of Vernon, Texas. At the young couple's earnest in-
sistence, the younger daughter lived with them until she was old
enough to get a job as clerk in a Vernon store.

Uncle Ike, as we always called him, was of even more restless
nature than my father. He was hardly old enough to join the
California gold rush but in the early 1850's left Missouri for
Kansas. Here he spent two or three years freighting merchandise
from the Missouri River ports to the little prairie towns before
returning to Missouri to get married and more or less settle
down.

To me, Uncle Ike was always a romantic and colorful figure.
Once he remarked to me, "Ed, I once boarded a couple of weeks
with old man Cody when his nephew, Willie, that was later
called 'Buffalo Bill,' was a little shirt-tail kid runnin' around th'
place."

With his two daughters living near Vernon, Texas, it was only
natural that Uncle Ike should drift out to that region. As he had
a big wagon and four good mules he had no difficulty in finding
profitable employment freighting goods from Vernon and

Quanah, Texas, to remote little towns that were forty to seventy
or more miles from the railroad. He usually returned with a load
of buffalo or cattle bones, which he sold at the railroad towns for
a good price.

For years he had no home except his covered wagon, in which
he slept on cold nights or when it was raining. In pleasant
weather he spread his blankets on the grass and slept under the
stars. Free and footloose, he visited his daughters for a day or so
and about once a year drove down to see us. To me he was a he-
roic figure coming, like young Lochinvar, out of the West.

On the occasion of his first visit, when I was about five years
old, I recall running out to meet him as his big wagon rolled to a
halt in front of our house. Then as I climbed up on the front
wheel of the wagon to shake his hand and peer back into the
cavernous depths of the space beneath its canvas cover, I felt that
I knew just how the West smelled! It smelled like a mixture of
Arbuckle coffee and brown sugar with a trace of the scent of
bacon, dried apples, sweating mules, and oiled harness leather,
all blended in a delightful odor which must be that of the West
itself!

Not only did Uncle Isaac keep us slightly in touch with the
Prairie West, but, as mentioned in a former chapter, my brother
Henry, before joining Mattie's husband in establishing a store,
came back to tell us of his work as a hunter, trapper, and Indian
trader. Then our father and Fannie's husband, Mace Hutchinson,
made their big trip to Navajoe, returning with stories of grass
almost waist high and level prairie land where one could plow a
furrow a mile or more long without encountering a single stone
or root.

Finally in October, 1888, Alice and I made the trip to Navajoe
to be followed by Father and George a month or so later. Perhaps my father would have remained in Greer County then, but
he would have had to settle on a claim near Navajoe and start
from scratch to impove it with very little money to make such
improvements.

When John and his wife, Ava, came down in the early spring
of 1890 to make a crop with us they brought us news of the
Navajoe region and the Dale clan living there. Henry had sold
his interest in the store and bought Jay's claim and built a new
house on it. He also was making other improvements, such as
planting more peach trees, thereby adding to the orchard which
Father had started on the place in 1889.

Henry's objective in adding two new rooms to the front of
Jay's half dugout became clear when, in the early spring of 1891,
he married sixteen-year-old Virginia White. She was a lovely
girl, the daughter of a prominent settler living about six miles
west of the little town of Navajoe. The forty-year-old husband
brought his bride to the "fashionable split-level" home he had
prepared for her, while Jay, who needed a farm about as much
as a Hottentot needs snow shoes, lived with John and Ava or
with Henry and his bride.

About 1891 we received a telegram telling us of the death of
our sister Alice at Henrietta, Texas. Around that same time Tom
and Lucy sold their Cross Timbers farm and removed to a rented
blackland prairie farm about three miles west of us. As this was
in easy walking distance we still visited them from time to time
but by no means as often as when they lived on the Cross Timbers
farm only a mile away.

In the meantime Uncle Isaac had married a widow who was running a boarding house in Vernon. He took his wife and her seven-year-old adopted daughter to a home that he had established about nine miles north of Navajoe near a country store and post office called Warren. Here my old uncle had built a commodious two-story house, had fenced fields and pastures, and had planted a large orchard.

It is not surprising that Father, with his brother, three of his sons, and his youngest daughter all living in Greer County, either in or near Navajoe, should begin to give serious consideration to leaving the little Cross Timbers farm and removing to Greer County, where a level prairie claim of 160 acres could be found near them. Perhaps even more important than this desire to be near his brother, sons, and daughter was Father's inborn love of pioneering.

Although he never spoke to George and me of our future, no doubt it was another factor in his decision to leave the Cross Timbers and remove to the Prairie West as soon as he could find a buyer for the little farm. By 1892 George was eighteen years old. This was an age when some Cross Timbers boys were at least beginning to think of getting married and establishing a home for themselves. While George had shown no signs of this he might do so at any time. In that event he would have to rent a small farm and become a tenant farmer, which was not a cheerful prospect. In the West he could have land of his own.

It seems to me now amazing that our father had been able to make a good living on our fifty-six–acre farm and also to save a considerable amount of money. There was no bank nearer than Fort Worth and few persons in our neighborhood had ever been inside a bank. Yet by 1892 my father had between three and four hundred dollars in gold coins stashed away behind the rafters of our attic bedroom.

It had been accumulated by hard work of all of us. Father was up at dawn every morning and called George and me before taking the milk buckets and heading for the cow lot to milk our three or four cows. By the time he had returned after straining the milk I usually had breakfast ready and George had the beds made and the house swept and cleaned up. After breakfast the dishes were quickly washed and put away in the safe and we were all ready for work. This was the order of the day when we were keeping "bachelor's hall." When John and Ava were with us for eight or nine months Ava, of course, did the cooking and other housework with a little help from her young sister, Minnie, and me.

As I look backward over a period of more than seventy-five years, it seems to me now that this home in the Texas Cross Timbers was an excellent place for a boy to grow up. Probably most social workers and amateur "do-gooders" of today would say that George and I were "underprivileged children." Maybe we were but we didn't *know it*. Nobody had ever told us that we were underprivileged and if anyone had we would have denied it bitterly.

It is true that our home had no bathtub or "outhouse" but neither did the home of any other family in our community. We bathed in a washtub on Saturday night, and when we went barefoot in the summer, washed our feet every night before going to bed. For women, the "bathroom" was under the bed or in the nearby thick woods of the hog pasture or behind the barn, corn crib, or tool shed. We had no heat in the house except what was furnished by the big fireplace in the front room and the cook stove in the kitchen. Obviously, we had no ice in the summer but the milk and butter were kept fairly cool in the cellar.

On the other hand, we had plenty of good food and a comfortable place to sleep at night, and, while we worked hard, we had plenty of time to play, hunt, fish, and visit with our friends and neighbors. It is true that as boys neither George nor I had much money to spend but we needed very little. I remember that Father once offered each of us a five-dollar gold piece, which we refused saying that we did not need any money!

All in all, life in the Cross Timbers was a very happy life. On the whole Father was not only better off financially than most of our neighbors but he was highly respected by everyone who knew him. I recall that upon one occasion two men came to ask him to join them in settling a controversy between two neighbors over a tract of land which both claimed to own.

Instead of "going to law" the two parties had agreed to settle the matter by each appointing one man and these two choosing a third. These three would then investigate the matter, hear the evidence, and render a decision, which both parties had agreed to accept as final. The two men appointed by the "litigants" had chosen my father as the third man to help them settle this question. This method of dealing with minor civil disputes had been used by the American pioneers as early as the occupation of the Virginia Piedmont by settlers and probably was as fair to the parties concerned as a more formal method would have been.

Upon another occasion, the son of a large landowner in the community brought a note from his mother asking my father to come over because "Family troubles are coming." Whether Father was able to help this family solve its domestic problems I do not know, but we never heard of any further difficulties.

Although Father's education was limited, it seems that he was regarded as a wise and fair-minded man by our neighbors in order to be asked to play the role of both judge and marriage counsellor.

Once the grapevine telegraph had spread the rumor that we were considering going to the West, the friends and neighbors did their best to discourage Father from leaving the Cross Timbers home. Here he was prosperous, comfortable, and among friends and church brothers. Why risk the hazards of moving to a distant Prairie West remote from a railroad and probably too dry to grow crops? Ever since early colonial days any man who migrated from a settled area to the thinly peopled West did so in spite of the advice and gloomy predictions of his more conservative neighbors.

Uncle Jack Clark was more philosophical in his comments. "If a man ain't sattyfide," he remarked to George and me, "I believe he should go to some place where he can be sattyfide. But I'm sattyfide. Got a good well o'water, twenty acres of good sandy land, makin' a good livin,' so I'm sattyfide."

One or two men came to see our father, apparently with some idea of buying our farm, but nothing came of their visits. Before the first one came, our father had consulted George and me as to what we should ask for the farm. He had earlier talked with us about selling the farm and going to Greer County and we had assured him that we were quite willing to go if he thought it best.

As to the price he should ask for the farm, he hoped to get eight hundred dollars but would take seven hundred, which we agreed was about right. Clearly Cross Timbers real estate was cheap enough!

It would never had occurred to George and me to question anything our father wanted to do but we both knew perfectly well that the time had come when he was eager to go to a new land. That his daughter, three sons, and brother were living in Greer County was not the only reason for his desire to go there. Perhaps of equal importance was his inborn restless pioneering spirit.

His amazing energy had enabled him to carve a productive little farm out of fifty-six acres of land covered with timber. He had cut all the timber except a ten-acre wood lot, used as a hog pasture; had split rails enough to enclose the fields; and had built, largely with his own hands, a comfortable log-and-lumber house of four rooms. In addition, he had built a cellar, a good barn, a corn crib, and a shed; had enclosed lots for the horses; and had planted a large orchard of peach, apple, and plum trees plus a quarter of an acre of blackberries and a large grape arbor.

All of this he had accomplished in about twelve years, for he had done considerable work on this little tract of land before moving onto it from the rented prairie farm. Now that he had done about all that he could to improve this farm, he doubtless felt that it was time to go farther west to a raw prairie land and repeat on a far larger scale the task of building a new farm home.

Some events and changes in the situation in the Navajoe region seemed to make our removal to that part of the Prairie West almost inevitable. On April 19, 1892, the huge Cheyenne and Arapaho Indian Reservation had been opened to settlement by homesteaders. Its southern boundary was only thirty miles north of Navajoe.

My brother Jay, who was always ready for any venture that promised excitement, made the race on horseback and staked a 160-acre claim on a little creek called Trail Elk. Unlike the rush at the opening of the Oklahoma lands three years earlier, in which almost every desirable 160-acre tract was occupied the first day, much of the western part of this reservation was not settled by homesteaders for three or four years.

Jay looked over the vacant land nearby and found a beautiful 160-acre tract only about a mile from his own claim. It was nearly all fertile valley land and had a small lake of perhaps an acre near the northeast corner, which may have been the reason why it had not been occupied by some homesteader. Due to Jay's urging, Henry had come to look at this tract of land and was so pleased with what he saw that he promptly filed on it as a homestead.

Henry was eager to get to work improving his new property as soon as possible. For this he would need some money. By this time he and his wife had a baby daughter and he did not like to leave them alone in their present home near Navajoe until he could get a new home built, a well dug, and other improvements made. He therefore offered to sell Father the place near Navajoe for $375 and proposed to bring Virginia and Baby Ora to stay with us on the Cross Timbers farm for a few months.

Father replied at once ageeing to buy the Navajoe claim at the price suggested and saying that we would gladly take care of his family for as long as necessary. It would be wonderful to have someone to cook and keep house for us again. Obviously we could not leave for the new home until the crops had been harvested, the livestock sold, and the farm either sold or rented to a good tenant.

Henry did not delay coming to us with his little family. We loved his wife, Virginia, whom we soon learned to call "Virgie" as Henry and apparently her own family did. Baby Ora was a lovely fat baby about five months old, who was very good, almost never cried, and required little attention.

Virgie was a very pleasant person, who quickly adjusted herself to what must at first have seemed a strange situation. Henry stayed only three or four days, as he was eager to get to work improving his new land. Father paid him part of the purchase price before he left and assured him that he would pay the remainder any time he needed it.

While $375 seems a small sum to pay for 160 acres of land with a three-room house, fenced fields, lots and sheds for the animals, plus a large orchard, it must be remembered that we were paying only for the improvements. There were many 160-acre tracts of equally good land upon which anyone could settle as a squatter, just as Jay had done soon after his return from Mexico.

That summer of 1892 was a busy one for all of us. Virgie came in June, when the blackberries were ripe. I remember that George and I picked forty gallons one day in ample time for our father to take them to town. The price of fruit and berries was very low as compared with that of today but so were prices of everything else. This included farm labor, for a good farm hand could be hired for a dollar a day or fifteen dollars a month, plus board.

We sold blackberries for twenty cents a gallon, peaches for a dollar a bushel for choice ones, and sweet potatoes for fifty cents a bushel. Because we had a very large peach crop that year, during threshing season Father was kept busy selling peaches to the wives of the prairie wheat growers. The small freestones and some of the smaller clingstone peaches that could not be sold, we dried. As a result, we had a thousand pounds of dried peaches when autumn came.

Virgie was an excellent cook, who also kept the house spotless, and washed and ironed all the linens, as well as our clothes and her own and Baby Ora's every week. As we had never been able to find good water on our farm we hauled water for household use from Uncle Jack Clark's well about a quarter of a mile east of our house. On washday in the summer, however, we found it easier to take the soiled linens and clothing to the well and wash them there.

As she had the baby to care for I usually helped Virgie with housework all I could by drying the dishes, churning, and doing other chores, including helping with the washing. In the summer, washing took a full half day in spite of the fact that Virgie had a great deal of energy and worked fast, although she was hardly more than a kid herself.

One washday in August will always remain green in my memory because it was my first, and last, time in my life to get gloriously drunk! Father and George were going to Keller, but before starting had taken Virgie and me together with the soiled clothes, washtubs, boiler, and such equipment over to Uncle Jack Clark's house. Here we set things up in a shady spot near the well.

For some reason we needed another tub and when Uncle Jack said there was one in the cellar I ran down the cellar steps to get it. The cellar floor felt refreshingly cool to my bare feet and in the dim light I saw that the tub had about four inches of water in it. As I picked up the tub a big copperhead snake coiled under it and struck me squarely on top of the foot.

I yelped, "Ouch! He bit me," and hastily carried the tub up the steps and set it down on the ground. He had hit me squarely on top of the foot and the blood was streaming up several inches high. I plunged my foot into the water in the tub and began to wash the wound.

Uncle Jack stood by helpless to do anything but heap maledictions on his snakeship's head, but my young sister-in-law was quick to go into action. She recalled that my father had recently bought a quart of whiskey, put it in a gallon jug, and added wild-cherry bark, bitter apple, stillingia roots, and prickly ashberries, among other ingredients, to make a vile-tasting bitters. He believed that a swallow of this every morning would help to ward off malaria.

Having always heard that whiskey was a sure cure for snake-bite, Virgie ran like a deer for home and raced back with this jug. Gasping for breath, she called for a teacup and poured it nearly full of this horrible mixture. "Now drink this right down, Ed," she ordered as, with a shaking hand, she passed the cup to me. I gulped it down, bad as it was. Then on the theory that if one cup would do *some* good two cups would do twice as much, she filled it again and once more I downed the evil-tasting liquid.

She and Mrs. Clark then demanded that I go into the house and lie down on the bed. Of course, in a few minutes the room began to whirl around. I dimly recall that Dow Taylor came into the room and I muttered to him, "Dow, I'm drunk." Then came complete oblivion until about sundown, when I awoke to see my father, George, and two or three other persons sitting by the bed.

Someone had gone to Keller to tell my father that his youngest son had been bitten by a deadly copperhead. He had brought a doctor out posthaste and rode with him in the buggy, leaving George to drive the wagon home. The medico took a good look at me and said, "Well, if the whiskey doesn't kill him, I'm sure he will be all right." The doctor was correct. They hauled me home in the wagon and my foot was sore for two or three days but that was all.

The remedy, however, probably affected my entire future life. It gave me such a distaste for alcohol that there has never been the slightest danger of my becoming an alcoholic or of my drinking too much. At a cocktail party, or any party where liquor is served, I will take one drink and sip it slowly all evening if possible.

It is my firm belief that if every thirteen-year-old boy could be induced to drink two cups of the type of bitters my father had in that jug, those who *lived* would never need to be warned to shun the "demon rum!"

When I was only about five years old someone had told me that my grandfather had been bitten by a snake when he was a small boy and that he carried the slow poison in his blood as long as he lived. The poison supposedly made the wound on his foot break out afresh every summer on about the date he was bitten and eventually caused his death! I recall feeling very sorry for my granddad until I learned that he died at the age of eighty-seven; the slow poison must have been very slow indeed!

Some six or seven weeks after my adventure with Mr. Copperhead, Henry wrote us that Virgie's mother was not too well and wanted Virgie to come back to her parents' home and stay with them until Henry could get their own home completed and they could move into it. He added that this would not be for several months. If we would put Virgie and Baby Ora on the train he would meet them at Vernon.

We missed Virgie and the baby a great deal at first, but since we were accustomed to running a "bachelor's hall" it was not too difficult to resume the practice of doing our own housework and cooking. Moreover, there was so much work to do that we had little time to be lonely. The corn must be gathered, the cotton picked, and the sweet potatoes dug. All these crops and the cows, pigs, and chickens must be sold. We shipped by freight to Vernon a few hundred pounds of dried peaches.

No buyer for the farm could be found, but it was at last rented to Mr. Beal, an elderly tenant farmer, who lived a few miles east of us. He was to pay a hundred dollars a year in cash rent instead of a share of the crops. Half of this was paid in advance, with the remainder to be paid the following autumn. He could not move in with his family until a few days after we had left, but our neighbor, Jake West, gladly agreed to look after the place until Mr. Beal came.

Because by this time the old musket was useless it was left in the attic, and George had sold the Kentucky squirrel rifle to one of the neighbors. This left us without a gun of any type, which to me was almost tragic, especially since were were starting for the West in a few days. I was therefore delighted when our father returned from a trip to Roanoke bringing me a twelve-gauge, single-barrel shotgun. Someone had left it at the grocery store to be sold and while it was far from new it was in good condition and the price was low.

Father could not have given me anything which would have pleased me as much as this gun. It was of the type called "Zulu," although just why is a mystery. Probably it was made from an army musket cut down about one half and fitted with a breech block, a new lock, and a shell ejector. If so, the idea may have originated in Europe and such guns traded to the Zulus of Africa for native products.

Obviously, this did not concern me. It was enough to know that I had my first breech-loading gun with a box of twenty-five cartridges and a complete reloading outfit. There was no doubt in my mind but that it would be possible to do a little hunting along the road west and that once we had reached our destination we would find prairie chickens, quail, and, on the Indian Reservation, wild turkeys and even deer and maybe bear that could be brought down with buckshot!

At long last came the day of departure. The day before the bows and canvas sheet had been put on the wagon, which had been carefully packed. Enough food had been put in a grub box for a couple of days, while a separate box held cooking utensils and dishes enough for the journey. The tools, bedding, surplus bedding, dishes, kitchenware, clothing, and jars of fruit, honey, and preserves had been packed in boxes and put in the rear of the wagon box.

I recall feeling glad that we were not leaving Texas, since Greer County had long been organized as a county of that state. Moreover, I had read Mrs. Pennybacker's *History of Texas* and had been thrilled by the deeds of Travis, Bowie, Crockett, Sam Houston, Deaf Smith, and all the other heroes of the Lone Star State. This heritage made me proud that I was the only one of my father's children to be born in Texas, the biggest state in the Union.

Old Turk could go west with us, but the cats were given to the Clarks, who were pestered by rats and mice. We could not take them and, besides, "it is bad luck to move cats." We had said good-bye to most of the neighbors the day before, but the Taylor boys, Paul and Dow, came over just as we had finished breakfast to bring us a "going-away gift" and wish us a happy journey.

We had known so long that we were going to our new home in the West that it is doubtful if any of us felt as much emotion in leaving the old one as he would if the decision to move had been a sudden one. Yet when the last package had been placed in the wagon I noticed that our father paused a moment to look over the entire little farm. Perhaps he was seeing in his mind's eye the fifty-six–acre tract of woodland which he had bought a dozen years before and was seeking to appraise what changes his labor had wrought.

Then we all shook hands with Paul and Dow, and Father climbed to the spring seat and picked up the lines. George

climbed up beside him and I took a seat on a roll of bedding just behind them with my cherished old Zulu carefully wrapped in a blanket beside me. Perhaps I had a little lump in my throat but I swallowed it as Father slapped the lines on the backs of the horses. Then with old Turk jumping about and barking gayly at the prospect of going somewhere, we headed westward and left the Cross Timbers forever.

INDEX

CPSIA information can be obtained
at www.ICGtesting.com
Printed in the USA
LVHW031120091221
705616LV00002B/31